WEBSTER'S WESTOWER ✓

Better
English
Grammar

D1407347

GEDDES & GROSSET

WEBSTER'S WORD POWER

Betty Kirkpatrick, a graduate of Edinburgh University, has a long career in reference publishing. She has edited *Chambers Twentieth Century Dictionary*, *Roget's Thesaurus*, the concise edition of *Brewer's Phrase and Fable*, and was language consultant to the *Encarta World English Dictionary*. She has compiled various other reference books, including the *Oxford Paperback Thesaurus* and the *Bloomsbury Dictionary of Clichés*. She acts as a consultant to the *Bloomsbury Good Word Guide*. Betty is author of an extensive list of publications on various aspects of the English language for learners of English.

Published 2014 by Geddes & Grosset, an imprint of
The Gresham Publishing Company Ltd.,
Academy Park, Building 4000, Gower Street,
Glasgow, G51 1PR, Scotland, UK

Copyright © 2014 The Gresham Publishing Company Ltd.

Text by Betty Kirkpatrick

ISBN: 978-1-84205-758-2

Printed and bound in Spain by Novoprint, S.A.

This book is not published by the original publishers of Webster's Dictionary or by their successors.

CONTENTS

WORDS THAT MAY CONFUSE

IDIOMS, CLICHÉS AND EVERYDAY PHRASES

BETTER ENGLISH GRAMMAR

Never has there been a greater need to make sure that you write and speak 'good' English. This is true of people in countries such as the UK where English is the native language and of people in countries where English is a second or foreign language. In countries where English is the language of business, a marked emphasis is now being placed on the need for competent communicative skills in the workplace. Although life in the modern world is generally less formal than it was and people in personal, academic and business contexts write considerably fewer letters than formerly, they are often still required to demonstrate their powers of written communication in the classroom and the workplace. For example, they might have to write a report for presentation to their work colleagues.

When it comes to correspondence, emails may have taken over from formal letters to a large extent but it reflects badly on a person if their emails are sloppily written and full of errors. The computer spell checker can only help you out to some extent. Many employers complain that a significant number of the people whom they recruit for jobs are sadly lacking in these skills. This is true even of young people who have just graduated from some of the top universities.

You might think that grammar and spelling are trivial matters, that they're just not that important in your line of work. You might think that as long as the facts are correct, what does it matter if the grammar is bad? However, poor grammar reflects badly on you—you might miss out on a job opportunity, you might not be taken seriously when making a complaint, you could even put off a potential Internet date—all because of terrible grammar and sloppy spelling. Any public display of poor language skills can give a very bad impression of even the most intelligent person.

At the same time, the importance of English as a world language continues to grow. In fact, there are many versions of Standard English spoken around the world: British, American, Canadian, Australian, Indian, South African, New Zealand and more. All have rich variations in vocabulary, syntax, semantics and grammar. More and more people in other countries are anxious to learn English and there is an ever-increasing demand both for teachers of English as a second or foreign language and for effective teaching materials in these areas.

But what is 'good' English or even correct English? Don't those of us who learn it as a native tongue at our mother's knee automatically speak and write it correctly? Alas, the answer to that is no. Native speakers obviously have much less of a struggle learning to speak good English than learners of English as a foreign or second language do, but the process is not effort-free.

Good or correct English is often regarded as grammatical English. Grammar has been variously described as the framework on which ideas are hung, and the cement that binds words together. Basically, grammar refers to the rules that govern the way a language works. Society cannot operate without rules and neither can language.

The prospect of learning grammar is more likely to depress those whose native tongue is English. Learners of English as a second or foreign language are used to having to come to grips with the grammar of their own languages and will not protest so much.

Often, the first time that people come into contact with written rules of grammar is when they come to learn a foreign language. The language is broken up into vocabulary, parts of speech, regular and irregular verbs, tenses, agreements and structures, etc. The rules of this foreign language seem more explicit, more 'grammatical' than that of our own, but, of course, our own language has such rules, it's just that we don't notice them.

It might be surprising to hear that, if your first language is English, you do already know some English grammar. You can speak the language, you understand others, you can respond and make yourself understood. For example, we automatically know the difference in structure between a question (Can I have that?) and a command (Give me that!).

You started to learn English grammar as an infant without consciously knowing you were doing so. You learned what were the correct structures and combinations of words through hearing others speak and—once you learned how to read—through the written word. Perhaps what you don't know about are the prescriptive rules that have been devised to describe English grammar. They used to be taught by rote in schools but emphasis on this side of teaching English has long since died out.

Spoken and written English are enormously different in structure and formality. Spoken discourse is often disjointed, with sentence fragments used in preference to complete sentences that would perhaps sound uncomfortably formal, yet it is easily understood. Even the world's most articulate and witty people do not always speak using perfect, prescriptively ordered, 'grammatically correct' English. Speech also employs stress, rhythm and intonation as an important part of conveying meaning.

However, our written words need structure and formality to convey meaning as accurately and unambiguously as possible; and our spoken words can still sound 'wrong' and give a bad impression if the formal rules are not followed.

Grammar has, over the years, got rather a bad press. At one point, in the UK, it was set aside by the educational powers-that-be as being largely unnecessary. Although it is now often seen as something valuable that should be brought back into prominence, it is also often seen as something essentially difficult and boring. This is not the case. It is logical and can be of great interest. Furthermore, you really have to get to grips with it if you want to improve your English.

In conclusion, in order to speak and write effectively and confidently in English, you must know something about the structure of the language. This book gives a clear explanation of the nuts and bolts of English grammar as well as hints on how to create a better personal writing style incorporating 'good' English.

WEBSTER'S WORD POWER

Betty Kirkpatrick, a graduate of Edinburgh University, has a long career in reference publishing. She has edited *Chambers Twentieth Century Dictionary, Roget's Thesaurus*, the concise edition of *Brewer's Phrase and Fable*, and was language consultant to the *Encarta World English Dictionary*. She has compiled various other reference books, including the *Oxford Paperback Thesaurus* and the *Bloomsbury Dictionary of Clichés*. She acts as a consultant to the *Bloomsbury Good Word Guide*. Betty is author of an extensive list of publications on various aspects of the English language for learners of English.

GRAMMAR

THE SENTENCE AND THE PARAGRAPH

The sentence

The most important unit of structure is the **sentence**. Most of the other grammatical units are parts that go together to form a sentence. However, that leaves us with the question 'What is a sentence?' and there has been some dispute about the definition. The traditional view of the sentence seems as good a jumping-off point as any—a unit of language that can stand alone and make sense.

The following are all complete in themselves, make sense and are, therefore, all sentences:

We ran.
The boy kicked the ball.
They played hard and they won.
Look over there!

Minor sentences

The following examples are also all complete in themselves and make sense and are, therefore, sentences. They are known as **minor sentences** or **irregular sentences**.

They are called **minor sentences** because they lack some of the other usual grammatical features of a sentence. For example, a minor sentence often lacks a **subject** and a **predicate** (*see* page 24).

Minor sentences are most common in spoken English and in conversation in literary fiction. They are also common in certain kinds of written English such as notices, labels and adverts. The following are examples of **minor sentences**:

No!
Nonsense!
How terrible!
What a view!
Good try!
No way!
Taxi!
Poison!
No entry.
Well done!
Once bitten, twice shy.

Major sentences

Other sentences are known as **major sentences** or **regular sentences**. A major sentence usually has a **subject** and **predicate** (*see* page 24). The following are examples of **major sentences**:

We ran.
The boy kicked the ball.
Mother baked a cake.
She leaves tomorrow.
They are coming to town.
She studied hard, but she failed the exam.
I called him when I arrived.

Subject and predicate

Basically, a sentence is a combination of two grammatical units—the **subject** and the **predicate**.

Subject

The **subject** of a sentence refers to what the sentence is about, often the person or thing that carries out the action of the verb. The **subject** usually gives a clear idea of what the sentence is about.

The subject can be a **noun**—either a **common noun** or a **proper noun** (*see* page 88) or a **verbal noun** (*see* page 90);
a **noun phrase** (*see* page 68);
a **pronoun** (*see* page 103);
a **subordinate clause** (*see* page 54);
an **infinitive** (*see* page 197).

In the following sentences the underlined words form the **subject** of the sentence and the subjects are **nouns**:

Dogs need a lot of exercise.
Children play in the park.
Money is extremely important to him.
Marriage is not for him, he says.
Accommodation is expensive in that area.
People are beginning to leave.
Jane is giving a party.
Jim has resigned.

Paris is the capital of France.
Mountaineering can be dangerous.
Dancing is her favourite pastime.
Painting can be a form of relaxation.

In the following sentences the underlined words form the **subject** of the sentence and the subjects are **noun phrases**:

A heatwave has been forecast.
Several unhappy employees have complained to the management.
The large black dog bounded up to the child.
Those terrible floods affected many people.
Representatives from the firm have issued a statement to staff.
James, my brother-in-law and dear friend, has just died.

In the following sentences the underlined words form the **subject** of the sentence and the subjects are **pronouns**:

They were found guilty.
We won the battle.
You have passed the exam.
He denied the charge.
She lost her wedding ring.
It has broken down again.

In the following sentences the underlined words form the **subject** of the sentence and the subjects are **subordinate clauses**:

Who she was remained a mystery.
Why he left has not yet been revealed.
What he says is not true.
When he will go has not yet been decided.

In the following sentences the underlined words form the **subject** of the sentence and the subjects are **infinitives**:

To do that would be unforgivable.
To get there is going to be very difficult.
To marry young is her main aim.
To get through your exams should be your principal concern.

NB: Dummy subject
A **dummy subject** sometimes has no intrinsic meaning but is inserted to maintain a balanced grammatical structure.
In the sentences

It has started to rain.
and
It is nearly midnight.
the word *It* is a **dummy subject**.

In the sentences

There is nothing else to say.
and
There is no reason for his behaviour.
the word *There* is a **dummy subject**.

NB: Directives

In sentences which are **directives** (*see* page 39) the subject often does not appear, but is implied, as in:

Get this out of here.
and
Lend me that pen for a minute, please.
The implied subject is *you*.

Predicate

The **predicate** refers to the part of a sentence or clause that gives information about the **subject**. It is basically all the parts of a clause or sentence that are not contained in the subject. It can either be a single verb or a number of elements.

Thus in the sentence
The little girl fell.
the word *fell* is the predicate of the sentence.

Similarly, in the sentence
The tired old man slept soundly.
the words *slept soundly* form the predicate of the sentence.

And in the sentencelog
The tired old man slept like a top.
The words *slept like a log* form the predicate of the sentence.

In the following sentences the underlined words form the **predicate** of the sentence:

Jane <u>fainted</u>.
Peter <u>was rich and powerful</u>.
Children <u>screamed loudly</u>.
The lights <u>went out all of a sudden</u>.
Workers <u>protested long and loudly at the factory gates</u>.
They <u>are leaving at the end of next week</u>.
We <u>took the stray kittens home</u>.
The students <u>celebrated their exam results all night long</u>.
The child <u>threw the red ball to the dog in the park</u>.

Object

Very often the **predicate** contains an **object**. The **object** of a sentence is the part of a sentence that is acted upon or is affected by the verb. It usually follows the verb to which it relates.

There are two possible forms of object in a sentence or clause—a **direct object** or an **indirect object**.

Direct object

A **direct object** refers to the person or thing that is directly affected by the action described by the verb.

The **direct object** can be a **noun**, and in the sentence
The girl hit the ball.
the word *ball* is a **noun** and the **direct object**.

A **direct object** can also be a **pronoun**, and in the sentence
She hit him.
the word *him* is a **pronoun** and the **direct object**.

A **direct object** can also be a **noun phrase**, and in the sentence
He has bought a large Victorian house.
the phrase *a large Victorian house* is a **noun phrase** and the **direct object**.

A **direct object** can be a **noun clause**, and in the sentence
I know what he means.
the clause *what he means* is a **noun clause** and the **direct object**.

In the following sentences the underlined words form a **direct object**:

The dog bit <u>the child</u>.
He dislikes <u>cats</u>.
We loved <u>them</u>.
People admire <u>her</u>.
He wanted <u>a comfortable city-centre flat</u>.

She lost <u>her diamond engagement ring</u>.
I don't know <u>what you mean</u>.
I asked <u>why you did that</u>.

Indirect object

An **indirect object** usually refers to the person who benefits from the action described by the verb, often by receiving something.

In the sentence
Her father sent the school a letter.
the school is the **indirect object** and *a letter* is the **direct object**.

NB: Direct and indirect objects
If there is a **direct object** and an **indirect object** in a sentence or clause, the **indirect object** is almost always placed before the **direct object**, as in:

I gave the boy the sweets.
where *the boy* is the **indirect object** and *the sweets* the **direct object**.

However, if both the **direct** and **indirect objects** are **pronouns** the **direct object** is sometimes placed first, especially in informal speech, as in:
That is my book. Give it to me, please.

NB: Verbs and indirect objects
Some verbs commonly take an **indirect object** as well as a **direct object**. These include **bring**, **buy**, **give**, **send**, **show**, **tell**.

In the following sentences the underlined words form an **indirect object**.

I sent <u>you</u> the book.
She showed <u>her mother</u> the letter.
We had to tell <u>her</u> the bad news.
They gave <u>the children</u> some sweets.
Mary bought <u>them</u> some magazines for the journey.
Pass <u>me</u> the salt, please.

An **indirect object** can be preceded by the word *to* or *for*.

So the sentence
Her sent the school a letter.
could be rephrased as
Her father sent a letter to the school.

And in this case the **direct object** would come before the **indirect object**.

Complement

In a sentence where the verb is a **linking verb** (*see* page 190), such as *be, become, seem,* etc, what follows the verb in a **predicate** is called not an **object,** but a **complement**.

In the sentence
Mark is a policeman.
the words *a policeman* form the **complement** of the sentence.

Similarly, in the sentence
Jane became a heart surgeon.
the words *a heart surgeon* form the **complement** of the sentence.

In the following sentences the underlined words form a **complement**:

He seems <u>an honest man</u>.
She became <u>a huge fan</u>.
They are <u>nice enough people</u>.
It appears <u>a good bargain</u>.

Punctuation of sentences

A sentence begins with a **capital letter** and ends with **a full stop** or an equivalent **punctuation mark** (*see* page 231), such as a question mark or exclamation mark.

Thus, the following are all sentences:

They did not like the house.
He lives in the country.
He designed and built the house.
We will leave when he gets here.
Where did he go?
Why did she leave?
Get out of here!
Help me!

(*See* pages 231–237.)

Types of sentence

Traditionally five types of sentence are recognized. These are **statements**, **negative sentences**, **questions**, **directives** or **commands** and **exclamations**.

Statements

Statements are sentences that 'state' something or give information. They are sometimes called **declarative sentences** because they 'declare' something. In most statements the subject comes before the verb. The following sentences are all **declarative sentences**:

The boy hit his sister.
The man thanked the old woman.
We serve evening meals.
The weather was dreadful.

Negative sentences

A **negative sentence** is one that makes a negative, rather than a positive, statement. This is usually created by the inclusion of a word such as *not*, *nothing* or *never*. The word *not* is sometimes contracted to *n't*. When *not* or *n't* is used it is accompanied by an **auxiliary verb** (*see* page 191). The following sentences are **negative sentences**:

We did not invite her.
I didn't see him.

I don't like it.
I don't know the man.
I heard nothing unusual last night.
They did nothing about it.
She has never been here.
We have never denied that.

NB: The double negative
The occurrence of two negative words in a sentence or clause is known as a **double negative**. If taken literally, this actually conveys the opposite sense to that which is intended.

Thus
He didn't say nothing.
literally conveys the idea that he said something.

However, this is rarely what is intended by the speaker or writer and the **double negative** should be avoided in standard English, although it is a feature of some regional dialects.
   Words such as *hardly* and *scarcely*, which can be regarded as semi-negative forms, are incorrectly used with a negative. When this happens it creates a double negative.

Thus, a sentence such as
We didn't hardly have time to catch the train.
is an example of incorrect usage.
You should say
We hardly had time to catch the train.

Questions

Questions are sentences that seek information of some kind. They are followed by a question mark (**?**) and they often involve the inversion of the subject and **an auxiliary** or **modal verb** (*see* pages 191, 194), as in:

Do you play the piano?
Did you pass the exam?
Have you written to him?
Didn't you like it?

There are three main types of questions: **yes-no questions**, **wh- questions** and **alternative questions**.

Yes-no questions

Yes-no questions are designed to seek a reply in the affirmative or negative, whether the reply is just 'yes' or 'no' or whether this is amplified in some way, as in:

Is the house occupied just now?
No.

Has the doctor arrived yet?
Yes. He's just arrived.

Are we ready to begin?
Let's get started. Yes.

Tag questions

Some **yes-no questions** are **tag questions** in which the questioning part is in the tag at the end of the sentence. The following are examples of tag questions, with the **tags** in bold:

*She's a lawyer, **isn't she?***
*He's not here yet, **is he?***
*You won't tell her, **will you?***

Wh- questions

Wh- questions begin with a word beginning with **wh**, such as *why, where, when, who* and *what,* as in:

What do you want?
Where did he go?
When did you last see her?
Who gave you that?

Alternative questions

Alternative questions require a reply that refers to the options given in the sentence. They contain the conjunction 'or'. The following are examples of **alternative questions**:

Did you come by bus or train?
By train.

Is the party on Friday or Saturday?
It's on Saturday.

Is she younger or older than him
She's a few years younger.

Exclamatory questions

Exclamatory questions are sentences which have the structure of questions but which are actually used as exclamations and end with an exclamation mark. They are really seeking the listener's agreement rather than seeking an answer. The following are examples of **exclamatory questions**:

Wasn't that a wonderful meal!
Hasn't she changed!
Isn't it a dreadful day!

Rhetorical questions

Rhetorical questions are also sentences that have the structure of questions and they end in a question mark. However, the speaker does not require an answer to these questions.

The following are examples of **rhetorical questions**:

Why should I care?
Who does she think she is?
How should I know?

Question by tone of voice

A **yes-no question** can have the structure of a statement, rather than a question, uttered in a questioning tone of voice and ending with a question mark.

The following are examples of this:

Anne told you I was going?
Yes, she did.

Tom has actually left already?
He went today. Yes.

The house is no longer for sale?
No. It's been sold.

Directives

Directives, which are also called **commands** (although they are not all actually commands), are sentences that instruct someone to do something.

In some **directives** an actual command is being given and this is followed by an exclamation mark, as in:

Keep quiet!

There is usually no subject in a directive and the verb is in its basic or infinitive form. In this kind of structure the verb is said to be in the **imperative mood** (*see* page 181).

The following are examples of **directives** in the **imperative mood**:

Stand up!
Help me, please!
Have a piece of cake.
Take two of these pills after meals.
Turn left here.

Some **directives** begin with the word 'let' or the word 'do', as in:

Let me help.
Let's go.
Do come in.
Don't worry.

Exclamations

Exclamations are sentences expressed by someone who is impressed, excited or roused by something. Exclamations sometimes take the form of a single word or a **minor sentence** (*see* page 22) but they can also be **major sentences**, often beginning with 'what' or 'how'. Exclamations always end with an exclamation mark (**!**).

The following are examples of **exclamations**:

Ouch!
What a day!
How pretty you look!

NB: Sentence length

As we have seen above, sentences, particularly minor sentences, can be extremely short. They can even be one word. On the other hand, sentences can be extremely long.

There is no restriction on the length of sentences, except, of course, that they should not be so long that they are confusing or unintelligible. Usually, relatively short sentences make for greater clarity. However, a series of sentences should not all be so short that the effect is too abrupt or jerky.

Apart from clarity, there is the question of style when it comes to sentence length. From the point of view of good style, it is important to vary the length of your sentences. A mixture of sentence lengths makes a piece of prose seem more interesting.

Kinds of sentence

Simple sentences

Short sentences often contain one **main clause** (*see* page 53) and a sentence with just one main clause is called a **simple sentence**.

The following are examples of **simple sentences**:

The boy laughed.
He enjoyed the trip.
We liked the play very much.
Her son is ill.
Her daughter became a doctor.
They gave me a present yesterday.

Multiple sentences

Sentences which contain more than one clause are known as **multiple sentences**, sometimes abbreviated to **multi-sentences**. These can either be **compound sentences** or **complex sentences**.

Compound sentences

Longer sentences usually contain more than one **clause**. Sometimes they consist of just two **main clauses** (*see* page 53), sometimes more than two. These clauses are linked by a **coordinating conjunction** (*see* page 217), such as *and*, *but* or *or,* and the sentences formed in this way are known as **compound sentences**.

The following are examples of **compound sentences**:

She loved the children and she looked after them well.
He left on time but the bus was late.
She will mend the dress or buy a new one.
I was sorry for him but I could not help him and I felt bad about that.
She played well but her opponent played even better and she lost the match.

Complex sentences

Longer sentences are often **complex sentences**. In **complex sentences** at least one of the clauses is a **main clause** but one or more of the clauses is a **subordinate clause** (*see* page 54).

A subordinate clause is connected to the main clause by a **subordinating conjunction** such as *although*, *because*, *before*, *since*, *unless*, *when*, *while* and *why*. Often the main clause comes before the subordinate, but sometimes the subordinate clause is put first.

The following are examples of **complex sentences**:

She danced while he played.
I left when they arrived.
The book was still where we had left it.
She cannot go unless her mother gives her permission.
Because his car broke down he arrived late at the wedding.
Wherever he goes, she goes.
Since you left he has been sad.

The paragraph

The **paragraph** is usually a considerably larger unit of structure than a **sentence**. Indeed, it usually consists of several sentences. Pieces of prose are usually divided into **paragraphs** to make the information conveyed by the prose more comprehensible and easier of access.

Unlike the construction of sentences, there are no set grammatical rules for the construction of paragraphs and many people find it difficult to divide their work into paragraphs. However, this improves with practice and soon becomes instinctive. Here are some guidelines.

There is no set length that a paragraph should be. A **paragraph** should deal with one particular theme or point of the writer's writing or argument. When that has been dealt with satisfactorily, a new paragraph should be started. If a paragraph is very long it can be difficult for readers to make their way through it and it can also be rather off-putting visually. In such cases it is best to consider subdividing the theme of the long paragraph to make shorter paragraphs.

On the other hand, it is best not to make all one's paragraphs too short as this can create a disjointed effect. Try to aim for a mixture of lengths to create some variety. Traditionally, it was frowned upon to have a one-sentence paragraph but there are no hard and fast rules about this. Usually, however, it takes more than one sentence to develop the theme of the paragraph, unless one is a tabloid journalist or copy-writer for an advertising firm.

The opening paragraph of a piece of writing should introduce the topic about which you are writing. The closing paragraph should sum up what you have been writing about.

New paragraphs begin on new lines and they are usually indented from the margin. In the case of dialogue in a work of fiction, each speaker's speech usually begins on a new line to make things clearer for the reader.

EXERCISES 1

1 Which of the following are **minor sentences**?

Have you finished?
Rubbish!
This food is tasteless.
How simply delicious!
What lovely flowers.
What's causing that dreadful smell?
No pain, no gain.
There is no smoke without fire.
Better luck next time.
No smoking.

2 Underline the **subject** in the following sentences.

They own several flats in the area.
Skating is her latest hobby.
Anne has got engaged to Peter.
To study hard should be your main concern.
There is no sense in this.
Where we go has not yet been decided.
It was a complete disaster.
Teachers from local schools protested against the school closures.
My cousin Jack works there.
Many disenchanted workers resigned right away.

3 Underline the **predicate** in the following sentences.

The old lady slipped on the ice.
He left suddenly without warning.
The soldiers moved slowly and cautiously.
The young man was on his best behaviour.
The lorry broke down yesterday on the motorway.
The teacher punished both pupils.
Jack happily invited them along.
She recovered from her cold quite quickly.
The heavy rain battered against the cottage windows all day and all night.

4 Which of the underlined words in the following sentences form **direct objects** and which form **indirect objects**?

The applicant gave <u>the official</u> the necessary information.
Each guest brought <u>a bottle of wine</u>.
She recognized <u>an old colleague</u>.
The child sent <u>her mother</u> a birthday card.
I know <u>what you mean</u>.
Pass <u>our guest</u> the bread, please.
She showed her friend <u>her new outfit</u>.
The result gave <u>the team</u> renewed confidence.
Send <u>me</u> the document, please.
We had to tell her <u>what happened</u>.

5 Which of the underlined words in the following sentences form **complements**?
They became <u>best friends</u>.

We made <u>great changes</u> to the system.
His friends blame <u>themselves</u>.
She seems <u>a very caring person</u>.
He appeared <u>as if from nowhere</u>.
Jack's father is <u>a professional tennis player</u>.
This looks exactly <u>what we need</u>.
She always gets <u>what she wants</u>.

6 Which of the following sentences are **negative sentences**?

We have something important to tell you.
I have never seen anything like it.
He didn't ever love her.
She saw something move the undergrowth.
It doesn't matter any more.
I know nothing about the incident.
They will mourn her forever.
We saw nothing in the least bit suspicious.
They weren't adequately equipped.
He did care for her once.

7 Replace the full stop with the appropriate punctuation mark at the end of any of the following sentences which are **questions**.

Where he went is a mystery to us all.
She has been gone a long time, hasn't she.
What did he say in reply.
Did she go abroad on holiday or stay at home.

When I last saw her she was very ill.
Is she older or younger than her sister.
Why she left so suddenly is unclear.
Have you lived here long.
The flat isn't very big, is it.
He'll come back one day, I'm sure.

8 Which of the following questions are likely to be **rhetorical questions**?

How can God do this to me?
Where is the nearest bus stop?
No one is serving me—am I invisible?
Do you know where we are?
Why does it always rain when I want to spend the day at the beach?
How does this machine work?

9 Which of the following sentences are **compound sentences** and which are **complex sentences**?

He enjoyed his work and he was very good at it.
While she was good at her work, she didn't enjoy it very much.
I won't go unless it stops raining.
We had intended going but it started to rain very heavily.
You can either study here or you can study in the library.
As it was getting late, we looked for somewhere to stay the night.
They can get the last bus or they can get a taxi.

If you miss the last bus you will have to get a taxi.
He's going to accept the dinner invitation, although he doesn't really want to go.

ANSWERS 1

1 *Rubbish!*
  How simply delicious!
  What lovely flowers.
  No pain, no gain.
  Better luck next time.
  No smoking.

2 *They own several flats in the area.*
  Skating is her latest hobby.
  Anne has got engaged to Peter.
  To study hard should be your main concern.
  There is no sense in this.
  Where we go has not yet been decided.
  It was a complete disaster.
  Teachers from local schools protested against the school closures.
  My cousin Jack works there.
  Many disenchanted workers resigned right away.

3 *The old lady slipped on the ice.*
  He left suddenly without warning.

The soldiers <u>moved slowly and cautiously</u>.
The young man <u>was violent and vindictive</u>.
The lorry <u>broke down yesterday on the motorway</u>.
The teacher <u>punished both pupils</u>.
Jack <u>quickly telephoned the police</u>.
She <u>recovered from her terrible injuries in time</u>.
The heavy rain <u>battered against the cottage windows
all day and all night</u>.

4 direct objects
   a bottle of wine, an old colleague, what you mean, the
   blood-stained knife, what happened.
   indirect objects
   the official, her mother, our guest, the team, me.

5 *best friends, a very caring person, a professional tennis*
   player, what we need.

6 *I have never seen anything like it.*
   He didn't ever love her.
   It doesn't matter any more.
   I know nothing about the incident.
   We saw nothing in the least bit suspicious.
   They weren't adequately equipped.

7 *She has been gone a long time, hasn't she?*
   What did he say in reply?
   Did she go abroad on holiday or stay at home?
   Is she older or younger than her sister?

Have you lived here long?
The flat isn't very big, is it?

8 *How can God do this to me?*
No one is serving me—am I invisible?
Why does it always rain when I want to spend the day at the beach?

9 **compound sentences**
He enjoyed his work and he was very good at it.
We had intended going, but it started to rain very heavily.
You can either study here or you can study in the library.
They can get the last bus or they can get a taxi.
complex sentences
While she was good at her work, she didn't enjoy it very much.
I won't go unless it stops raining.
As it was getting late, we looked for somewhere to stay the night.
If you miss the last bus you will have to get a taxi.
He's going to accept the dinner invitation, although he doesn't really want to go.

CLAUSES, PHRASES AND PHRASAL VERBS

Clauses

A clause, like a **major sentence**, is a meaningful group of words containing a **subject** and **predicate** (*see* page 24). However, unlike sentences, not all clauses can stand alone and make sense.

Main clause

A clause that can stand alone and make sense is known as a **main clause**. Every major sentence must have at least one main clause. (*See* **Types of sentence** page 34). In each of the following sentences the underlined words form a **main clause**:

He was at the office *when I arrived*.
I knew *why he left*.
We took the train *because the car broke down*.

Some sentences consist of more than one **main clause** connected by a **coordinating conjunction** (*see* page 217) such as *and*, *but* or *or*. Such sentences are known as **compound sentences** (*see* page 42).
The following sentences consist of two **main clauses**:

I was very angry and he knew it.
You can either apologize or you can leave immediately.
It was a sunny day but it was very cold.

The following sentences consist of more than two **main clauses**:

*She was intelligent and she was very efficient but she had
no luck in finding a job.*
*We can get a flight today or we can get one next week, but
we cannot get one at the weekend.*

Punctuation and main clauses

A **comma** may be used to separate **main clauses**
joined by a **coordinating conjunction** (*see* page 217),
but this is not usual, especially if the clauses have the
same subject and the coordinating conjunction is
and. When the coordinating conjunction is *but*, the
use of a comma to mark off the main clause is more
a matter of choice, especially when both clauses are
quite long.

Subordinate clause

A clause that cannot stand alone and make sense and
is dependent on the main clause to make sense is
called a **subordinate clause**. A subordinate clause can
come before or after a main clause. In each of the
following sentences the underlined words form a
subordinate clause.

He arrived <u>after we had started the meal</u>.
*We won't be able to put in an offer for the house <u>until we
sell our own</u>.*

He failed the exam <u>although he worked hard</u>.
<u>If you buy that car</u> you will regret it.
<u>When he saw her</u> he smiled.
I wonder <u>why she left</u>.

There are several types of **subordinate clause**. With the exception of a verb, a subordinate clause can replace most elements of a sentence (adverb, adjective and noun).

Adverbial clause

A subordinate **adverbial clause** performs a similar function to an adverb in a sentence.

For example in the sentence
She left for the airport early.
the word *early* is an adverb.

This adverb can be replaced by an adverbial clause, as in:
She left for the airport <u>when it became light</u>.
or
She left for the airport <u>before the city traffic got too heavy</u>.

In both these sentences the underlined words form an adverbial clause.

In some cases an **adverbial clause** can come before the main clause, as in:
Before he left he gave her a letter.

If the **adverbial clause** comes before the main clause it is sometimes separated from the main clause by a comma, especially when the adverbial clause is quite a long one. When the adverbial clause follows the main clause there is usually no comma. *See* **Commas and subordinate clauses** page 247.

Types of adverbial clause

There are various types of **adverb** (*see* page 209) and, correspondingly, there are various types of **adverbial clause**.

adverbial clause of time
This indicates the time something happens and is introduced by a **conjunction** (*see* page 217) relating to time such as *after, before, when, whenever, while, until, as soon as*.

   The words underlined in each of the following sentences form an **adverbial clause of time**:

We need to leave <u>before the traffic gets bad</u>.
He got there <u>as I was leaving</u>.
It had snowed heavily <u>while we slept</u>.
<u>Whenever they meet</u> they quarrel.
<u>While we slept</u> someone broke into the house.

adverbial clause of place
This indicates the place that something happens and is introduced by a **conjunction** (*see* page 217) relating to place such as *where, wherever, everywhere*.

The words underlined in each of the following sentences form an **adverbial clause of place**:

We left the books <u>where we had found them</u>.
<u>Wherever we went</u> we saw signs of terrible poverty.
<u>Everywhere she goes</u> she upsets people.

NB: Conjunctions and relative clauses
If the conjunctions *where* or *when* follow a noun the subordinate clause so formed is <u>not</u> an adverbial clause of place, but a **relative clause** (*see* **Relative clause** page 61). For *where* you can substitute *in which* and for *when* you can substitute *at which*. In each of the following sentences the underlined words form a **relative clause** <u>not</u> an **adverbial clause**.

This is the place <u>where we last saw him</u>.
This is the time <u>when the pain gets worse</u>.

---

adverbial clause of purpose
This indicates the intention someone has when doing something and is introduced by a **conjunction** (*see* page 217) relating to purpose such as *in order (to)*, *to*, *so as to*, *so that*.

The words underlined in each of the following sentences form an **adverbial clause of purpose**:

We started on our journey very early <u>so that we could avoid the city rush hour</u>.

In order to pass the exam you are going to have to work a lot harder.

He reduced the number of staff *in order that he might avoid bankruptcy*.

We are saving hard *so that we can buy a new house*.

adverbial clause of reason

This indicates why something happens or is done and is introduced by a **conjunction** (*see* page 217) relating to reason such as *because, since, as, in case*. The words underlined in the following sentences form **adverbial clauses of reason**:

I couldn't go to the wedding *because I had to work that day*.

As it was raining we had the party indoors instead of in the garden.

Since your child broke the window you should pay for the repair.

I'm taking some sandwiches *in case there is no buffet on the train*.

adverbial clause of result

This indicates the result of an event or situation and is introduced by a **conjunction** (*see* page 217) relating to result, *so that*. The words *so* and *that* can be separated, *so* coming before an adjective or adverb in the main clause and *that* being the first word in the subordinate clause. The words underlined in each of the following sentences form an **adverbial clause of result**:

She spoke very quickly <u>so that we could scarcely understand her instructions</u>.
He fell awkwardly <u>so that he broke his leg</u>.
She was <u>so</u> ill <u>that she had to be taken to hospital immediately</u>.
We were <u>so</u> bored <u>that we left the lecture early</u>.

An **adverbial clause of result** always comes after the main clause, unlike some other adverbial clauses which can also come before it.

adverbial clause of condition
This indicates a possible situation and its consequences and is introduced by a **conjunction** (*see* page 217) relating to condition such as *unless, if, as if, provided (that), providing, as long as*.

The words underlined in each of the following sentences form an **adverbial clause of condition**:

I'll come to the party <u>provided I don't have to work</u>.
<u>If you finish your project</u> you can leave early.
I could have told you that <u>if you had bothered to ask me</u>.
We will miss the plane <u>unless we leave for the airport now</u>.
<u>As long as you work late this evening</u> you can have tomorrow morning off.
<u>If you study hard and do well in your exams</u>, you will easily get into university.

adverbial clause of manner
This indicates the way someone behaves or the way in

which something is done, and is introduced by a **conjunction** (*see* page 217) relating to manner such as *as though, as if, as, like*.

The words underlined in each of the following sentences form an **adverbial clause of manner**.

He talks <u>as if he knows a lot about the subject</u>.
She looked at him <u>as though she hated him</u>.
Why does he behave <u>as he does</u>?

An **adverbial clause of manner** always follows the main clause, unlike some other adverbial clauses which can also come before it.

adverbial clause of concession
This contains a fact that contrasts in some way with the main clause or makes it seem surprising and is introduced by a **conjunction** (*see* page 217) such as *although, though, even though, whereas, while, whilst*. The words underlined in each of the following sentences form an **adverbial clause of concession**:

I admire his work <u>although I don't really like him</u>.
<u>Even though she loves him</u> she doesn't trust him.
<u>Whilst he works very hard</u>, he doesn't really achieve anything.
My friend loves to lie on the beach all day, <u>whereas I like to explore the surrounding villages</u>.

Although he had all the right qualifications and experience for that particular post, he was not appointed.

Comparative clause

A **comparative clause** is a subordinate clause that modifies comparative adjectives and adverbs and is introduced by *than*. The words underlined in each of the following sentences form a **comparative clause**:

The task was much more difficult than any of us had anticipated.
He worked harder than we could ever have imagined.
The writer looked a lot younger than I had imagined her to be.

Relative clause

A **relative clause** performs a similar function to an adjective in a sentence. It comes immediately after a noun in the main clause, which is called the **antecedent**, and gives more information about this noun. A relative clause is introduced by a **relative pronoun** (*see* pages 62, 116), such as *who*, *whose*, *which* and *that*, and this comes immediately after the **antecedent**. *Who* and *whom* are used when the noun refers to a **person**, *which* is used when it refers to a **thing** and *that* can be used of either a person or thing. *Whom* is used when the relative pronoun is the object of the verb in the relative clause. *Whose* is used when you want to refer to something relating to the person or thing you are talking about. The words underlined in each of the sentences below form a **relative clause**.

That's the boy <u>who built the bike</u>.
I know the man <u>whose wife was a surgeon</u>.
These are the men <u>whose wages have been increased</u>.
It is a country <u>whose population is in decline</u>.
He is the neighbour <u>whom we like best</u>.
Here is the book <u>that I borrowed</u>.
I lost the ring <u>which he gave me</u>.
He reported the driver <u>that damaged his car</u>.

Sometimes the **relative clause** divides the parts of a **main clause** rather than coming after it. The words underlined in each of the sentences below form a **relative clause**:

The house <u>that we liked most</u> was much too expensive for us.
The woman <u>whose daughter is ill</u> is very upset.
The dream <u>which I had last night</u> was very vivid.

NB: Relative pronoun
Sometimes there is no relative pronoun at the beginning of the relative clause, as in the underlined clauses below:

He was the best cook <u>we ever had</u>.
She was not then the rich woman <u>she later became</u>.
He wasn't the man <u>she thought he was</u>.

NB: Of which
In formal English, especially written English, *of which* is sometimes used instead of *whose*, as in the underlined clauses below:

It is one of those cities <u>of which the centre has become a slum</u>.
The ruined castle is one of those buildings <u>of which the history is inadequately documented</u>.

Types of relative clause

There are two types of **relative clause**. A **defining relative clause** identifies which person or thing you are talking about.

Defining relative clause
The words underlined in each of the following sentences form a **defining relative clause**:

I recognized the woman <u>who stole my purse</u>.
There is the man <u>whom she adores</u>.
He bought the necklace <u>which she had admired</u>.
These are the chocolates <u>that Mum likes best</u>.

Non-defining relative clause
A **non-defining relative clause** is not needed to identify the person or thing that you are talking about, but it gives further information about that person or thing.

The words underlined in each of the following sentences form a **non-defining relative clause**:

They walked down the town's main street <u>which was called George Street</u>.
He fell in love with the girl next door <u>who became his wife</u>.
He got his promotion <u>which was long overdue</u>.

Punctuation in relative clauses

Where a **non-defining relative clause** divides the parts of a main clause it is placed within **commas**.

His two sisters, <u>who were very close to him</u>, never got over his death.
The old man, <u>who is nearly 90</u>, has become the oldest person to complete a marathon.

Commas are not used in this way in the case of **defining relative clauses**.

The book <u>that he took</u> was very valuable.
The car <u>that we bought</u> proved to be unreliable.

Prepositions in relative clauses

When there is a preposition in a relative clause this is often placed at the end of the clause, which is often also the end of the sentence. Previously it was considered a grammatical error to end a sentence with a preposition, but this attitude has changed. However, the preposition <u>can</u> be put in front of the relative pronoun as long as the sentence so formed sounds natural. This is most often done in formal English, particularly written English.

This is what has happened to the society <u>which we live in</u>.
or
This is what has happened to the society <u>in which we live</u>.

Unbelievably, he has given up the job <u>which he trained so hard for</u>.
or
Unbelievably, he has given up the job <u>for which he trained so hard</u>.

This is the kind of behaviour <u>that I refuse to put up with</u>.

You would NEVER say:
This is the kind of behaviour <u>up with which I refuse to put</u>.

Noun clause or nominal clause

A **noun** or **nominal clause** performs a similar function to a noun or noun phrase in a sentence. Like a noun it can act as the **subject**, **object** or **complement** (*see* pages 24–32) of the main clause.

The words underlined in each of the following sentences are noun clauses that act as the **subject** of the sentence:

Where you go is of very little interest to me.
What you know should be told to the police.
What he does now is up to him.

The words underlined in each of the following sentences are noun clauses that act as the **object** of the sentence:

I'm not asking why you're going.
We didn't know who had done it.
He refused to say where he was going.

The words underlined in each of the following sentences are noun clauses that act as the **complement** of the sentence:

The theory is that there will definitely be enough money for everyone.
My point is that we simply can't afford to move house.

NB: Nouns and prepositions
Sometimes noun clauses come after a preposition. The words underlined in each of the following sentences are noun clauses:

It depends on how much money is available.
They all commented on what a lot of weight he had lost.

Comment clause

A **comment clause** is a short clause inserted into a sentence, sometimes used to show the speaker's attitude to what he or she is saying and sometimes used as a filler without much meaning. Comment clauses are particularly common in informal speech.

The words underlined in each of the following sentences form a **comment clause**.

To put it bluntly, he is a liar.
He wasn't sent to prison for the crime, more's the pity.
The patient will most likely survive, I'm glad to say.
She's only a few years older than me, you know.
He's been married twice before, it seems.

NB: Use of a comma
A **comment clause** is often separated from the main clause by a **comma.**

Phrases

A **phrase** usually refers to a group of words that work together to form a grammatical unit, although, in fact, a phrase may consist of just one word.

A clause or sentence can usually be broken down into phrases. There are five kinds of phrase and each phrase takes its name from the word class (*see* pages 87–199) which plays the main part in its structure.

Thus, in a **noun phrase** a noun is the main part of the structure of the phrase and in an **adjective phrase** an adjective is the main part of the structure of the phrase.

Noun phrase

A **noun phrase**, also called a **nominal phrase**, is a group of related words in which the main word is a noun and which functions like a noun in a sentence or clause. Thus, *a very long black car* is a noun phrase in which the main word is the noun **car**.

A noun phrase can either act as the **subject**, **object** or **complement** of the sentence or clause. The words underlined in each of the following sentences are all noun phrases.

In the first two sentences the noun phrases act as the **subject**:

The most wonderful thing has happened.
A terrible storm is forecast.

In the next two sentences the noun phrases act as the **object**:

We have some interesting new neighbours.
I met a very charming woman at the party.

And in the last two sentences the noun phrases act as the **complement**:

His father is a fairly talented artist.
My great-aunt later became a famous opera singer.

Adjective phrase

An **adjective phrase**, also called an **adjectival phrase**, is a group of related words in which the main word is an adjective and which functions like an adjective in a sentence or clause. Thus, *rather too old* is an adjectival phrases in which the main word is the adjective **old**. The words underlined in each of the following sentences are **adjective phrases**:

She was <u>tired, miserable and hungry</u>.
The task was <u>extremely challenging</u>.
The patient was getting <u>paler and weaker</u>.
The flowers were <u>fresh from the garden</u>.
On the day of the picnic the weather was <u>the worst possible</u>.

Adverb phrase

An **adverb phrase**, also called an **adverbial phrase** or an **adverbial**, is a group of related words in which the main word is an adverb and which functions like an adverb in a sentence or clause.

Thus,

extremely frequently

is an adverb phrase in which the main word is the adverb *frequently*.

The words underlined in each of the following sentences are **adverb phrases**:

I used to play tennis <u>fairly regularly</u>.
I saw both of them <u>very recently</u>.
I can't stand this noise <u>for much longer</u>.
She greeted her guests <u>extremely warmly</u>.
The students are working <u>really hard</u>.
They live <u>very close</u>.

Preposition phrase

A **preposition phrase**, also called a **prepositional phrase**, is a group of related words in which the main word is a preposition and which functions like a preposition in a sentence or clause.

Thus

on the table

is a preposition phrase in which the main word is the preposition *on*.

The words underlined in each of the following sentences are **preposition phrases**:

We waited <u>at the bus stop</u>.
He placed the book <u>on the table</u>.
They walked <u>into the room</u>.
You must stay <u>in the garden</u>.

Participial phrase

A **participial phrase** is a group of related words in which the main word is a participle of a verb, either a **present participle**, as in the following sentence:

<u>*Walking*</u> *along the beach, he thought deeply about his problems.*

Or a **past participle**, as in the sentence:

Disgusted by her treatment, she resigned from her job.

The words underlined in the following sentences are **participial phrases**:

Bored by the party, she went home early.
Living by himself, he was frequently lonely.
Relieved by the news, he smiled broadly.
Laughing happily, she went off to celebrate.
Built by his father, the house had been designed by him.
Weeping bitterly, the child held the broken toy.
Destroyed by war-time bombing, the city is now being rebuilt.
Badly injured, the miners somehow managed to make their way to the surface.
Deeply touched by the gesture, the young woman wrote a thank you-note.

Phrasal verbs

A **phrasal verb** is a verb that consists of two or three words. They can consist of a verb followed by an adverb *or* they can consist of a verb followed by a preposition *or* they can consist of a verb followed by an adverb and a preposition.

Examples of **phrasal verbs** are shown in the sentences below with the **phrasal verb** underlined.

In this first group of sentences the **phrasal verbs** all consist of a verb followed by an **adverb**:

We sat down and waited.
She slipped on the ice and fell over.
They set off just before dawn.
When does the plane take off?
It's time to go in.
The price of property here will go up.
Come up now, please.
How long did it take for the patient to come round?
Winter will set in soon.
The effects of the painkiller began to wear off.
Our holiday plans have fallen through.
Lie down and try to sleep.
The car had moved off.
He hopes to find a permanent job and settle down.
The child curled up and went to sleep.
The caller rang off before I got to the phone.

In the next group of sentences the **phrasal verbs** all consist of a verb followed by a **preposition**:

They <u>walked through</u> the forest.
We <u>drove through</u> the city at midnight.
You should <u>call on</u> your new neighbour.
The child <u>fell into</u> the water.
My father finally <u>got over</u> his illness.
The workers <u>asked for</u> more money.
He originally <u>came from</u> London.
She <u>was living with</u> her parents at the time.
We <u>had pored over</u> all the holiday brochures.
He <u>is embarking on</u> a new career.
We <u>banked on</u> your support.
She <u>brought up</u> her children alone.
He <u>turned down</u> the job offer.

In this last group of sentences the **phrasal verbs** all consist of a verb followed by an **adverb** and a **preposition**.

Tiredness <u>crept up on</u> her as she drove and she decided to stop for some coffee.
We'll have to <u>come up with</u> another source of funding.
It is time they <u>did away with</u> these out-dated laws.
He must <u>face up to</u> the possible consequences of his action.
I refuse to <u>put up with</u> our noisy neighbours any longer.
You are bound to <u>come up against</u> a few problems in the course of this task.

She <u>looked up to</u> her father until she discovered that he was a crook.

The children <u>get up to</u> a lot of mischievous tricks when the teacher leaves the room.

He <u>ran off with</u> his best friend's wife.

It all <u>comes down to</u> money in the end.

Position of object in phrasal verbs

Many phrasal verbs act like intransitive verbs (*see* page 187). Some, however, act like transitive verbs and, as such, take a **direct object** (*see* page 28).

When a phrasal verb is used in a transitive situation you sometimes have a choice as to where to place the object. If it consists of a short noun phrase, the object can be placed either after the second word of the phrasal verb, or after the first word and before the second word. In the following sentences the underlined words, in different positions, represent the object:

We filled up <u>the water jug</u> with cold water from the kitchen tap.

or

We filled <u>the water jug</u> up with cold water from the kitchen tap.

He'll never live down <u>this terrible scandal</u>.

or

He'll never live <u>this terrible scandal</u> down.

The quarrel tore apart <u>the entire family</u>.
or
The quarrel tore <u>the entire family</u> apart.

When the object is a **pronoun**, such as *him*, *her*, *it*, it usually comes before the second word of the phrasal verb.

In the following sentences the underlined words form phrasal verbs and their pronoun objects:

I gave my letter of complaint to the manager, but she immediately <u>handed it over</u> to her assistant.
When she broke off the engagement he wanted her to keep the ring, but she <u>gave it back</u>.
It was Jim who thought of the idea, but it was Jack who <u>put it forward</u> to the committee.
The little girl was badly injured and police are trying to find the driver who <u>knocked her over</u>.
The young boxer was knocked out and doctors took several minutes to <u>bring him round</u>.

NB: Dangling participle

A **dangling participle** is a **participle** (*see* page 198) that has been misplaced in a sentence. A participle is often used to introduce a phrase that is attached to a subject mentioned later in a sentence as in:

Worn out by the long walk, she fell to the ground in a faint.

Worn out is the participle and *she* the subject.

It is a common error for such a participle not to be related to any subject, as in:

Working mainly at night, it seemed along time since she had seen daylight.

This participle is said to be 'dangling'.

Another example of a **dangling participle** is contained in

Living alone, the days seemed long.

where *Living alone* is not related to a particular subject.

It is also a common error for a participle to be related to the wrong subject in a sentence, as in:

Painting the ceiling, some of the plaster fell on his head.

Painting is the participle and should go with a subject such as *he*. Instead it goes with *some of the plaster*.

Participles in this situation are more correctly known as **misrelated participles**, although they are also called **dangling participles**.

EXERCISES 2

1 Underline the **subordinate clauses** in the following sentences.

No one knew who she was.
They left before the rush hour got under way in earnest.
There is the youth who stole my purse.
Doctors won't know his chances of recovery until they get the test results.
As the sun continued to shine we decided to stay at the beach a little longer.
That is the book that I have been looking for.
If you leave now you will be there by nightfall.
The drains get blocked whenever it rains heavily.
She acts as if she were superior to the rest of us.
She didn't tell him when she would be back.

2 Write down which type of **adverbial clause** (i.e. time, place, reason, etc) is underlined in the following sentences.

Because the tickets were so expensive I didn't go to the concert.
He is moving to this area in order to be nearer his work.
The ring will be where you left it.
He walked so quickly that I had difficulty in keeping up with him.
As long as we get him to a hospital right away he should be all right.
She's going to buy the dress although she can't afford it.

The rent of the flat was much more expensive <u>than I had anticipated</u>.

3 Underline the **relative clauses** in the following sentences.

She is one of those mothers who overprotect their children.
That is the name of the man whose car I bought.
He bought the cottage which my aunt used to own.
This is the dress that she likes best.
The village is the place where we first met.
Jack was the friend whom my father trusted most.
She was not the honest woman that we all considered her to be.
That was the moment when she fell in love.
It is one of those areas in which the population has declined rapidly.

4 Which of the following **relative clauses** are **defining** and which are **non-defining**?

She bought the flowers <u>which were her mother's favourites</u>.
We went to the exhibition at the city portrait gallery <u>which is in Queen Street</u>.
That is the teacher <u>who teaches my son maths.</u>
His birth mother, <u>whom he finally tracked down</u>, did not want to know him.
They had dinner at the town's best fish restaurant <u>which is quite near where they live</u>.

We eventually bought the house <u>which we had seen first</u>.
The students <u>who passed the exam</u> were all in the top section of the class.
This is the area <u>where most people want to live</u>.
My former neighbour, <u>who moved away a few years ago</u>, died last week.

5 Write out the sentences which contain a **noun clause** and underline that clause.

The police suspected that she was the thief.
We knew who committed the crime.
They are the people who really care.
We realize that it is not your fault.
Where he goes every night no one knows.
This is the place where they meet.
I'm not telling you when I plan to leave.
That was the day when his exam results were due.
His theory is that they'll come round eventually.

6 Underline the **comment clauses** in the following sentences.

To be frank about it, I wouldn't believe a word he says.
We have to move to the city, I'm sorry to say.
The police arrested the wrong man, it appears.
To be realistic, I think the job will take at least six weeks.

7 Write down which of the following underlined phrases are **noun phrases**, which are **adjectival phrases** and which are **adverbial phrases**.

A _terrible accident_ occurred last night.
The weather was _wet, windy and bitterly cold_.
They worked _rapidly and competently_.
We saw _some wonderful scenery_.
I once knew them _very well indeed_.
She drove _quickly and carelessly_.
The young woman was _beautiful, slender and well-dressed_.
She married _a handsome but untrustworthy man_.

8 Underline the **participial phrases** in the following sentences.

Smiling happily, she congratulated the young couple on their engagement.
She ran along the road, shouting loudly.
Completely exhausted by the day's work, she had a bath and went to bed early.
Savagely bombed by enemy aircraft, the area was a wilderness for many years.
Greatly amused by the speech, the crowd applauded enthusiastically.
Designed and made by her mother, the dress attracted a great deal of admiration.

Walking slowly and painfully, I eventually reached the doctor's surgery.

9 Underline the **phrasal verbs** in the following sentences.

They stood up and applauded warmly.
I fell over the cat.
The dog lay down by the fire.
Our neighbours are moving away.
He comes from London originally.
She asked for more time to pay.
Our guests set off after dinner.
I can't put up with this noise any longer.
They brought up their children in extreme poverty.
The plane will take off shortly.
The effects of the sleeping pills wore off slowly.

ANSWERS 2

1 *No one knew <u>who she was</u>.*
They left <u>before the rush hour got under way in earnest</u>.
There is the youth <u>who stole my purse</u>.
Doctors won't know his chances of recovery <u>until they get the test results</u>.
<u>As the sun continued to shine</u> we decided to stay at the beach a little longer.
That is the book <u>that I have been looking for</u>.
<u>If you leave now</u> you will be there by nightfall.
The drains get blocked <u>whenever it rains heavily</u>.
She acts <u>as if she were superior to the rest of us</u>.
She didn't tell him <u>when she would be back</u>,

2 *<u>Because the tickets were so expensive</u> (**reason**)*
*<u>in order to be nearer his work</u> (**purpose**)*
*<u>where you left it</u> (**place**)*
*<u>that I had difficulty in keeping up with him</u> (**result**)*
*<u>As long as we get him to a hospital right away</u> (**condition**)*
*<u>although she can't afford it</u> (**concession**)*
*<u>than I had anticipated</u> (**comparative**)*

3 *She is one of those mothers <u>who overprotect their children</u>.*
That is the name of the man <u>whose car I bought</u>.

He bought the cottage <u>which my aunt used to own</u>.
This is the dress <u>that she likes best</u>.
The village is the place <u>where we first met</u>.
Jack was the friend <u>whom my father trusted most</u>.
She was not the honest woman <u>that we all considered
her to be</u>.
That was the moment <u>when she fell in love</u>.
It is one of those areas <u>in which the population has
declined rapidly</u>.

4 <u>which were her mother's favourites</u> (*defining*)
<u>which is in Queen Street</u> (*non-defining*)
<u>who teaches my son maths</u> (*defining*)
<u>whom he finally tracked down</u> (*non-defining*)
<u>which is quite near where they live</u> (*non-defining*)
<u>which we had seen first</u> (*defining*)
<u>who passed the exam</u> (*defining*)
<u>where most people want to live</u> (*defining*)
<u>who moved away a few years ago</u> (*non-defining*)

5 The police suspected <u>that she was the thief</u>.
We knew <u>who committed the crime</u>.
We realize <u>that it is not your fault</u>.
<u>Where he goes every night</u> no one knows.
I'm not telling you <u>when I plan to leave</u>.
His theory is <u>that they'll come round eventually</u>.

6 <u>To be frank about it</u>, I wouldn't believe a word he says.

We have to move to the city, <u>*I'm sorry to say*</u>.
The police arrested the wrong man, <u>*it appears*</u>.
<u>*To be realistic*</u>, I think the job will take at least six weeks.

7 A <u>terrible accident</u> occurred last night. *(noun phrase)*
The weather was <u>wet, windy and bitterly cold</u>. *(adjectival phrase)*
They worked <u>rapidly and competently</u>. *(adverbial phrase)*
We saw <u>some wonderful scenery</u>. *(noun phrase)*
I once knew them <u>very well indeed</u>. *(adverbial phrase)*
She drove <u>quickly and carelessly</u>. *(adverbial phrase)*
The young woman was <u>beautiful, slender and well-dressed</u>. *(adjectival phrase)*
She married <u>a handsome but untrustworthy man</u>. *(noun phrase)*

8 <u>Smiling happily</u>, she congratulated the young couple on their engagement.
She ran along the road, <u>shouting loudly</u>.
<u>Completely exhausted</u>, she had a bath and went to bed early.
<u>Savagely bombed by enemy aircraft</u>, the area was a wilderness for many years.
<u>Greatly amused by the speech</u>, the crowd applauded enthusiastically.
<u>Designed and made by her mother</u>, the dress attracted a great deal of admiration.

<u>*Walking slowly and painfully,*</u> *I eventually reached the doctor's surgery.*

9 *They <u>stood up</u> and applauded warmly.*
I <u>fell over</u> the cat.
The dog <u>lay down</u> by the fire.
Our neighbours <u>are moving away</u>.
He <u>comes from</u> London originally.
She <u>asked for</u> more time to pay.
Our guests <u>set off</u> after dinner.
I can't <u>put up with</u> this noise any longer.
They <u>brought up</u> their children in extreme poverty.
The plane will <u>take off</u> shortly.
The effects of the sleeping pills <u>wore off</u> slowly.

PARTS OF SPEECH I

Main parts of speech

The smallest unit of language is the **word**. In grammar each word is assigned a grammatical category known as a **part of speech**.

The following main parts of speech are discussed in this section: **noun, pronoun, adjective, determiner, verb, adverb, preposition** and **conjunction**.

Nouns

Often called a 'naming word' in primary schools, a **noun** is used to refer to a person, thing or quality. Nouns are a very common feature of language and they are categorized into various classifications as follows.

Common and proper nouns

A **common noun** refers to something of which there are many examples and so is very common. The following words are examples of **common nouns**:

apple, band, car, city, country, day, dog, man, month, planet, religion, street.

A **proper noun**, on the other hand, refers to something in particular of which there is only one example. Unlike common nouns, **proper nouns** begin with a capital letter. Thus, the following words are examples of **proper nouns**:

Granny Smith (type of apple), Beatles (name of pop group), Buddhism, Volkswagen (trade name of type of car), London, Sweden, Wednesday, Doberman (type of dog), Jack (name of man), March, Mars (name of planet), Scotland Street.

Concrete and abstract nouns

A **concrete noun** refers to something that you can touch. The following are examples of **concrete nouns**:

bag, carpet, door, flower, grape, hand, lake, monkey, orange, pan, road, shoe, window.

An **abstract noun** refers to something that you cannot touch. In other words, it refers to a quality, concept or idea. The following are examples of **abstract nouns**.

anger, beauty, Christianity, courage, danger, fear, greed, happiness, loyalty, Marxism, wisdom, youth.

Countable and uncountable nouns

A **countable noun**, also known as a **count noun**, is a noun that can be preceded by the word 'a' and can exist in a plural form. When the plural form is used it is not usually preceded by a determiner, but is used alone. Most **concrete nouns** are countable. The following are examples of **countable nouns**:

city (plural cities), gate (plural gates), foot (plural feet), hat (plural hats), lady (plural ladies), monkey (plural monkeys), mouse (plural mice), taxi (plural taxis), window (plural windows).

In the following sentences the underlined words, either in the singular or plural form, are **countable nouns**:

I've just bought a <u>flat</u> there.
I prefer <u>cities</u> to the countryside.
Open the <u>door</u> please.
The child believes in <u>fairies</u>.

The <u>church</u> is over there.
There are <u>mice</u> in the house.

An **uncountable noun**, also known as an **uncount noun**, is a noun that cannot usually be preceded by the word 'a' or 'an' and does not usually exist in a plural form. Abstract nouns tend to be uncountable. The following are examples of **uncountable nouns**:

They lived in <u>poverty</u>.
Our <u>luggage</u> went missing.
We are waiting for vital <u>information</u>.
You should put <u>sugar</u> in this pudding.
<u>Education</u> is an obsession with her.
I put some <u>petrol</u> in the car yesterday.
I'll have a kilo of <u>flour</u>, please.
Could I have a slice of <u>bread</u>?

Verbal noun

When the **present participle** (*see* page 198) functions as a noun it is known as a **verbal noun** or **gerund**. The **verbal noun** is so called because, although formed from a verb, it functions as a **noun**, acting as the subject of a sentence. In the following sentences the underlined words are **verbal nouns** or **gerunds**:

<u>Smoking</u> is bad for your health.
<u>Stealing</u> is a crime.
<u>Jogging</u> is good exercise.
<u>Swimming</u> is his favourite sport.

NB: Countable and uncountable nouns
Some nouns exist in both countable and uncountable forms. One example is the word *cake* which is **countable** in the example
The child ate three cakes.
and **uncountable** in the example
Do have some cake.

Another example is the word *light* which is **countable** in the example
The lights in the house suddenly went out.
and **uncountable** in the example
She was depressed by the lack of light in the winter.

In some situations it is possible to have a **countable** version of what is usually an **uncountable** noun. Thus, although the word *sugar* is usually considered **uncountable**, as in the example
Add a little sugar to the mixture.
it can be used colloquially as a **countable noun** in the example
I take two sugars (= teaspoonfuls of sugar).

Similarly, although the word *tea* is usually considered **uncountable**, as in the examples
I would love a cup of tea.
and
She invited me to tea.
Tea can be used colloquially as a **countable noun** in the example
I'll have two teas without sugar, please.

Sometimes the **verbal noun** can act as the object of a sentence. In the following sentences the underlined words are **verbal nouns** or **gerunds** acting as the object of a sentence.

I don't enjoy <u>swimming</u>.
She hates <u>dancing</u>.
She gave up <u>smoking</u>.
He took up <u>jogging</u> in the park.
They loathe <u>eating</u> in restaurants.
The young men love <u>drinking</u> in pubs.
She took to <u>giving</u> noisy parties late at night.

Nouns or pronouns that qualify **verbal nouns** or **gerunds** should be in the **possessive case** (*see* pages 103–110, 134, 146, 295), as in:

My mother hates <u>my</u> smoking in her house.
and
The head teacher objected to <u>our</u> wearing casual clothes on the school trip.

In these sentences the words *my* and *our* are both in the possessive case.

However, there is a general tendency to think of gerunds as being a very difficult area of the English language. The result is that most people do not understand that the gerund should be preceded by a noun or pronoun in the possessive case and they, instead, use an **object**, as in:

My mother hates me smoking in her house.
and
The head teacher objected to us wearing casual clothes on the school trip.

Although ungrammatical, such usage is becoming more and more common.

Collective nouns

A **collective noun** is a singular noun that refers to a group of things or people when the whole group is being considered. In the following phrases the under-lined word is a **collective noun**:

a pack of wolves
a flock of sheep
a herd of cattle
a school of whales
a shoal of herring
a fleet of ships
a pride of lions
a swarm of flies
a gaggle of geese
a constellation of stars.

Singular and plural forms of nouns

Regular singular forms of nouns

Most English nouns have a different ending for 'one' of something (called the **singular** form) than they do for 'more than one' (called the **plural** form). In the case of the majority of nouns the plural is formed regularly simply by adding *s* or *es* to the singular, as in *bat/bats, monkey/monkeys, church/churches*. In cases where the singular noun ends in a consonant followed by *y* then the plural form regularly becomes *ies*, as in *fairy/fairies*.

Regular plural forms of nouns

The following is a list of common nouns with their **regular plural forms**:

banana	*bananas*
berry	*berries*
bush	*bushes*
dog	*dogs*
elephant	*elephants*
friend	*friends*
house	*houses*
kiss	*kisses*
lady	*ladies*
march	*marches*
porch	*porches*
road	*roads*
story	*stories*
table	*tables*
taxi	*taxis*
umbrella	*umbrellas*
variety	*varieties.*

Irregular plural forms of nouns

Some nouns do not form their plural in the above regular ways. Instead their plural forms are said to be irregular.

Some **irregular plurals** are formed, not by adding an ending to the singular form, but by changing the vowel in the singular forms, as in *man/men,* or by having a completely different form from the singular, as in *mouse/mice.*

The following are examples of nouns with their **irregular plural forms**:

foot	*feet*
goose	*geese*
tooth	*teeth*
woman	*women.*

A few **irregular plural forms** are formed by adding 'en' to the singular form, as in *ox/oxen.* In the case of the word *child* the letter *r* is added before the *en.*

Some nouns ending in *f* form **irregular plurals** ending in *ves,* as in *loaf/loaves.* The following is a list of such nouns with their plural forms:

half	*halves*
leaf	*leaves*
scarf	*scarves*
wife	*wives*
wolf	*wolves.*

NB: Irregular and regular forms
The word *hoof* can either have the **irregular plural form** *hooves* or the regular plural form *hoofs*. The word *roof* usually has the regular plural form *roofs*.

Foreign plural forms of nouns

Some nouns in English have a plural form that follows the spelling rules of the foreign language from which they are derived, as in *stimulus* (*stimuli*). The following are examples of such words with the plural form in their original foreign language:

bacterium	*bacteria*
bacillus	*bacilli*
criterion	*criteria*
larva	*larvae*
phenomenon	*phenomena*.

Unchanging plural form

Some **irregular plural forms** are the same as the singular form of the noun. These include *sheep, salmon* and *grouse* (the game bird).

Nouns used only in the plural form

There are some words, such as *jeans, scissors* and *trousers*, which are only used in the plural form and

NB: Foreign plurals

In modern English there is a tendency to anglicize the plural forms of foreign words. Many of these co-exist with the original foreign plural form, as *thesaurus (thesauri/thesauruses)*. Other examples include *formula (formulae/formulas), appendix (appendices/appendixes), index (indices/indexes)* and *gateau (gateaux/gateaus)*.

In the case of the words *appendix* and *index* the two plural forms are used in different contexts. The plural *appendices* is used in a literary context, as in the *appendices* added as additional information to a book, whereas the plural *appendixes* is used in a medical context, as in the surgical removal of *appendixes*. The plural *indices* is usually used in a mathematical context, whereas the plural *indexes* is usually used in a literary context to refer to a guide to a book.

have no singular equivalent form. To refer to any of these in the singular the construction *a pair of jeans, scissors* or *trousers* is used.

Gender of nouns

Many languages, such as French and German, are affected by the concept of grammatical gender. Thus, in French the word *hill* is feminine (*la colline*) according to grammatical gender, although in gender in the real world it would be neuter. Similarly, the German word for a mountain (*der Berg*) is masculine in terms of grammatical gender, although in the real world it is neuter.

This is not true of English because English nouns tend to be grouped according to the natural distinctions of sex, or, where appropriate, absence of sex. Thus, we have the gender categories of **masculine, feminine** and **neuter** and a *man* or *boy* is classified as **masculine**, a *girl* or *woman* is classified as **feminine** and a *table* or *chair* as **neuter**.

The words in the following list are masculine:

bridegroom, brother, duke, drake, emperor, father, husband, king, nephew, prince, son, widower.

The words in the following list are the feminine equivalents of the words in the masculine list:

bride, sister, duchess, duck, empress, mother, wife, queen, niece, princess, daughter, widow.

The words in the following list are neuter:

apple, bottle, car, desk, egg, house, letter, newspaper, road, shoe, town, window.

Dual gender

Some nouns in English, such as *child*, can either refer to a male or a female, unless the sex is indicated in the context. The words in the following list fall into this category:

adult, architect, artist, athlete, baby, author, cousin, doctor, parent, secretary, singer, student, teacher.

Feminine forms

Some words in the dual gender category, such as *author, poet, sculptor and proprietor*, were formerly automatically assumed to be masculine and they had feminine forms, as in *authoress, poetess, sculptress* and *proprietrix*. The rise of the Women's Movement in the 1960s with its concern for the equality of women in society gave rise to a corresponding concern for sexism in language. Words such as *authoress* and *poetess* were thought to be sexist and are now generally thought to be unacceptable. However, some feminine forms, such as *waitress*, are still in common use and both *actor* and *actress* are used for a female actor.

Person in compound nouns

The need to remove sexism from language also resulted in the increase in use of the word **person** to form compounds that could refer to either a man or a woman and were, therefore, of dual gender. Such words include *chairperson* and *spokesperson*. These replaced *chairman* and *spokesman* which were hitherto thought to be able to apply to a man or a woman, although they sounded masculine.

(*See* **he** under **Pronoun**, page 107.)

Compound nouns

Many nouns, known as **compound nouns**, consist of **two** or more **words**. A compound noun is a fixed expression that is made up of more than one word and functions as a noun in a sentence or clause. Most compound nouns consist of two **nouns** or an **adjective** and a **noun**, but some, such as *cover-up* and *make-up*, are derived from **phrasal verbs** (*see* page 73) and some, such as *passer-by* and *looker-on*, are derived from a **noun** plus **adverb**. A few compound nouns consist of a letter of the alphabet and a noun, as in *X-ray* and *U-turn*.

Some **compound nouns** are written as **two words**, as in *estate agent*, some are separated by a **hyphen**, as in *pen-friend*, and some are written as **one word**, as in *housewife*. Sometimes which style of writing you use for compound nouns is a matter of choice. For example, *baby-sitter* can also be written as *babysitter* and *spin-off* can be written as *spinoff*. If you want to be consistent in your writing, it is best to select a reliable dictionary and follow its recommendations.

The words in the following list are all examples of **compound nouns**:

air conditioning, bank account, blood pressure, coffee jug, doorstep, fairy tale, frying pan, health centre, housewife, income tax, letter-box, make-up, musical instrument, nail varnish, passer-by, police station, seaweed, swimming pool, teapot, washing machine.

Plural forms of compound nouns

The plural forms of **compound nouns** vary according to the type of words they are made up of. If the final word of a compound noun is a countable noun, the plural form of the countable noun is used when the compound noun is made plural, as in *swimming pools*, *police stations, letter-boxes* and *coffee jugs*.

Compound nouns that are directly derived from **phrasal verbs** (*see* page 73) usually have a plural form ending in *s*, as in *cover-up/cover-ups* and *show-off/ show-offs*.

In the case of **compound nouns** which consist of a **count noun** and an **adverb** the plural form of the noun is used before the adverb when the compound noun is in the plural form, as in *passers-by* and *lookers-on*.

Nouns and noun phrases in apposition

A noun or noun phrase is said to be **in apposition** when it is placed next to another noun or noun phrase and provides further information about it, especially by saying something that identifies or describes it. In such a situation, the main noun or phrase and the amplifying noun or phrase refer to the same person or thing. In the following sentences the underlined words are **in apposition**:

My eldest brother, <u>the acting head of the firm</u>, has called a shareholder meeting.

My nearest neighbour, <u>the owner of Grange Farm</u>, has kindly offered to check in on my house while I am away. George Jones, <u>a well-known local lawyer</u>, is standing in the local council elections.

The man who caused all this trouble, <u>the children's father</u>, has walked away without punishment.

For punctuation *see* **The comma with nouns or phrases in apposition** on page 252.

Pronouns

A **pronoun** is a word that takes the place of a noun or noun phrase in a sentence.

In the following sentences the underlined word is a **pronoun**:

I bought an apple and ate <u>it</u>.
I phoned Jane and invited <u>her</u> to dinner.
<u>*You*</u> *should have asked permission.*
Jack told Sally all about <u>himself</u>.
Is <u>anyone</u> there?
<u>*Who*</u> *said that?*
<u>*Those*</u> *are gloves.*
<u>*Each*</u> *of us had to sing a song.*
He thanked the man <u>who</u> had saved his life.

There are several types of **pronoun** and they are categorized as follows.

Personal pronouns

A **personal pronoun** is a pronoun that is used to refer back to someone or something that has already been mentioned. Of the different kinds of pronoun the **personal pronouns** are the most common.

There are three types of **personal pronoun**, according to their function in the sentence. The **subject pronoun** is used as the subject of a sentence; the **object pronoun** is used as the object of a sentence; the **possessive pronoun** is used to indicate that a person or thing belongs to, or is associated with, another person or thing. In sentence *1* below, the underlined word is a personal **subject pronoun**, in sentence *2* the underlined word is a personal **object pronoun** and in sentence *3* the underlined word is a **possessive pronoun**.

1 *I looked after the children.*
2 *The grandparents looked after her.*
3 *That car is mine.*

I and we: the first person personal pronoun

Personal pronouns are also categorized according to **person**.

The **first person personal pronoun** refers to the person who is speaking or writing when referring to himself or herself. The **first person personal pronoun**, in the singular form, is *I* and, in the plural form, *we*, when it acts as the subject of a sentence. When it is the object of a sentence the singular form is *me* and the plural form is *us*. The **possessive** form of the first person personal pronoun in the singular form is *mine* and in the plural form is *ours*.

In the following sentences the underlined words are **first person personal pronouns** acting as the subject of the sentences:

She said, 'I am going home.'
'I am going shopping,' he said.
'We have very little money left,' she said to her husband.
He said, 'We shall have to leave now if we are to get there on time.'

In the following sentences the underlined words are **first person personal pronouns** acting as the object of the sentences:

'I think he hates <u>me</u>,' Jane said.
'It's obvious that she deceived <u>us</u>,' said Jim.
'You have been very kind to <u>me</u>,' said Sue.

In the following examples the underlined words are **first person personal pronouns**, in the possessive form also known as **possessive pronouns**:

'That book is <u>mine</u>,' said Anne.
'We won,' said Bill, 'and so the prize is clearly <u>ours</u>.'

You: the second person personal pronoun

The **second person personal pronoun** refers to the person or thing that is being addressed in the sentence. The **second person personal pronoun** is *you*, whether it is the pronoun or object of the sentence and whether it is singular or plural. Unlike in some languages, the **second person personal pronoun** does not alter its form in English. The **possessive** form of the second person personal pronoun is *yours* in both singular and plural forms.

In the following sentences the underlined words are **second person personal pronouns** acting as the subject of the sentences:

<u>*You*</u> *should have told me earlier, Jane.*
<u>*You*</u>*, Mum and Dad, have been very generous to me.*
<u>*You*</u> *all are equally to blame.*

NB: Me and I

Many people are confused about when to use *I* and when to use *me*. It is often wrongly assumed that the use of the word *me* is less polite than that that of the word *I*.

In fact, the pronoun *I* should be used as the subject of a sentence, as in:
Jim and I are going on holiday together.
or
May Jane and I come to the party?

The pronoun *me* should be used as the object of a sentence, as in:
They invited my brother and me to tea.
or
They played tennis against my father and me.

Exception Except in very formal contexts, it is now considered quite acceptable to say.
It is me.
although, strictly speaking, this use is ungrammatical and it should be
It is I.
However, this sounds very stilted and it is rarely used.

In the following sentences the underlined words are **second person personal pronouns** acting as the object of the sentences:

NB: Between, I and Me
There is some confusion as to whether the preposition *between* should be followed by *I* or *me*. Because *between* is followed by an object, the correct answer is *me*, as
The dog stood between me and the gate.
or
There is a great deal of ill feeling between my cousin and me.
It is wrongly assumed that the use of *me* is less polite than that of *I*.

Someone has called <u>you</u>.
I blame <u>you</u> for what happened, Jim.
Your mother loves <u>you</u> both equally.

In the following sentences the underlined words are **second person personal pronouns** in the possessive form. These are also known as **possessive pronouns**.

This pen is <u>yours</u>, Jim, is it?
Sue and Sally, the prize is <u>yours</u>.
Is this dog <u>yours</u>, Mr and Mrs Jones?

He, she, it and they: the third person personal pronoun

The **third person personal pronoun** refers to a third party, not to the speaker or writer of the sentence or to the person being addressed. The **third person personal pronouns** are, in the singular form, *he, she* and *it* and, in the plural form, *they*, when the personal pronoun is the subject of the sentence. When the **third person personal pronoun** is the object of the sentence it takes the form of *him, her* or *it* in the singular form and, in the plural form, *them*. The possessive forms of the **third person personal pronoun** in the singular are respectively *his, hers* or *its*. In the plural the possessive from is *theirs*.

In the following sentences the underlined words are **third person personal pronouns** acting as the subject of the sentence:

<u>He</u> left school last year.
<u>She</u> is the youngest of the three sisters.
<u>It</u> was the only hotel with vacancies in the area.

In the following sentences the underlined words are **third person personal pronouns** acting as the object of the sentence:

Jane met <u>him</u> at a party.
I drove <u>her</u> to the station.
The house was charming and we loved <u>it</u> at first sight.

In the following sentences the underlined words are **third person personal pronouns** in the possessive form. They are also known as **possessive pronouns**.

The stolen car is <u>theirs</u>.
The fault is <u>theirs</u>, apparently.
That part of the garden is <u>theirs</u>.

NB: Personal pronouns and sexist language
Until fairly recently, it was very common to use a masculine personal pronoun to refer to a noun where the gender was not known, as in:

If a student does not attend classes regularly he will be asked to leave college.

or

If the applicant is successful he will be expected to start the job next week.

When the movement towards the removal of sexist language from the English language began, this use of *he* was considered to be sexist and such sentences required to be rephrased.

The problem is that this is not easy to do. Where possible, the easiest way of doing this may be to turn the whole sentence into the plural, as in:

If students do not attend classes regularly they will be asked to leave college.

Alternatively, the easiest course of action may be to use 'he or she' or 'he/she' instead of *he*, as

If the applicant is successful he or she (he/she) will be expected to start work next week.

This last way round the problem is felt by many people to be clumsy, particularly in spoken or informal English. The solution often used now is ungrammatical in nature. Thus, instead of using 'he/she' many people use 'they' instead, although the rest of the sentence is left in the singular form. Instead of saying

Every student has been instructed that he/she must register for the exams by the end of December.

they say

Every student has been instructed that they must register for the exams by the end of December.

The use of the third person personal pronoun in plural form in such contexts is becoming more and more common, frequently being used in textbooks and dictionaries and even more so in newspapers, magazines and works of fiction.

Possessive pronouns

Possessive pronouns *see* **first person personal pronouns, second personal pronouns** and **third personal pronouns**, pages 103–110.

Reflexive pronouns

Reflexive pronouns end in -*self* or -*selves* and refer back to a noun or pronoun that has been mentioned earlier in the sentence. The following is a list of **reflexive pronouns**:

myself, ourselves, yourself, yourselves, himself, herself, itself, themselves.

In the following sentences the underlined words are reflexive pronouns:

I cut <u>myself</u> with the breadknife.
You will have to wash <u>yourself</u> in cold water.
He sees <u>himself</u> becoming a lawyer.
The cat was licking <u>itself</u>.
The town's inhabitants braced <u>themselves</u> for the storm.

Reflexive pronouns can also be used for emphasis, as in the following sentences:

The town <u>itself</u> is not very attractive, but the surrounding countryside is beautiful.
The headmaster <u>himself</u> decided on the boys' punishment.
We <u>ourselves</u> must provide the funding for the project.

NB: Emphatic pronouns
Reflexive pronouns which are used, as above, for emphasis are sometimes known as **emphatic pronouns**.

Reflexive pronouns can also be used to indicate that someone has done something alone without the help of anyone else, as in:

The bride made that beautiful dress herself.
The young couple are planning to build the house themselves.
I'm sure that he did not write that book himself.

Reciprocal pronouns

Reciprocal pronouns are pronouns which are used to indicate a two-way relationship or to convey the idea of reciprocity. The **reciprocal pronouns** are *each other* and *one another*. In the following sentences the underlined words form **reciprocal pronouns**:

The two sisters have hated <u>each other</u> from childhood.
It is important to help <u>each other</u> as much as possible.
The children are always calling <u>one another</u> unpleasant names.
The friends helped <u>one another</u> with their geography homework.

Demonstrative pronouns

Demonstrative pronouns are used to indicate or point to things or people. The **demonstrative pronouns** are *this, that, these* and *those*.

The **demonstrative pronouns** *this* and *these* are used to refer to something or someone close to the writer or speaker, while *that* and *those* are used to refer to something further away. In the following sentences the underlined words are **demonstrative pronouns**:

I'm sure <u>this</u> is my book.
<u>This</u> is my father.
<u>That</u> is definitely Dad's car.
<u>That</u> is my cousin.

These are my favourite flowers.
These are my nephews, Jim and John.
These are some of the issues which we will be discussing this term.
Those are very expensive houses.
Those were interesting points which you raised at the meeting.
Those are our nearest neighbours.

Indefinite pronouns

Indefinite pronouns are pronouns that are used to refer to people or things without specifying exactly who or what they are. The following is a list of the **indefinite pronouns**:

anyone, anybody, anything, everyone, everybody, everything, someone, somebody, something, no one, nobody, nothing.

> **NB: No one**
> Unlike the other **indefinite pronouns** *no one* is written as two words.

In the following sentences the underlined words form an **indefinite pronoun**:

Is anyone there?
I don't know anybody here.
I didn't buy anything.
Does everyone have a drink?

Nothing matters now.
Everybody knows at least one other person here.
She has everything she could ever want.
Someone must know what happened.
No one can help me now.
I know somebody who can help.
I have something to tell you.
Nobody understands.

Some other pronouns are sometimes classified as **indefinite pronouns**. *See* **distributive pronouns** below.

Distributive pronouns

Some pronouns were traditionally known as **distributive pronouns** but are now also variously known as **indefinite pronouns** (*see* above) or **universal pronouns**. Often such pronouns are followed by an 'of' construction. The following is a list of such pronouns:

all, both, each, either, neither, more, most, some.

In the following sentences the underlined words are **distributive/indefinite/universal pronouns**:

We thought a few workers would be declared redundant, but, in the end, all kept their jobs.
All of the victims of the crash survived.
The three boys were involved in the crime and each deserves to be punished.

Each of the girls stands a chance of winning the competition.

I am very impressed by these two projects and think that either of them would suit our purpose well.

Neither of the candidates seemed suitable for the job.

There are too many student applicants for the college positions available and some will be disappointed.

Interrogative pronouns

Interrogative pronouns are pronouns which are used to ask questions. They are among words sometimes called **wh- words** because they all begin with the letters 'wh-'. The following is a list of **interrogative pronouns**:

who, whom, to whom, whose, which, what.

Who is used as the subject of an **interrogative sentence**, while the **object** in formal or written English is *whom*. In informal or spoken English the **object** of an **interrogative sentence** is often *who*. The **interrogative pronoun** *to whom* is confined to formal or written English.

In the following sentences the underlined words are **interrogative pronouns**:

Who has got the job?
Whom did she blame?
Whom did he appoint as his heir?

To whom was he referring?
Whose is the blue car?
Which of these do you prefer?
What happened then?

See **interrogative adverbs**, page 213.

Relative pronouns

Relative pronouns are pronouns that introduce a **relative clause** (*see* page 61). The **relative pronoun** refers back to a noun or noun phrase in the main clause, called the **antecedent**. In each case the **antecedent** is the word immediately before the relative pronoun. The following is a list of **relative pronouns**:

who, whom, whose, which, that.

In the following sentences the underlined words are **relative pronouns**:

There's the man <u>who</u> stole the car.
She was the only person <u>whom</u> I could trust.
That's the man <u>whose</u> permission we need for the project to go ahead.
This is the last house <u>which</u> he built.
The dress <u>that</u> I would like is too expensive.

EXERCISES 3

1 Which of the following nouns are **proper nouns** and so should be spelt with a capital letter?

lion, child, tuesday, book, october, castle, venus, america, region, mount everest, day, sunshine, uncle william, ocean, new york, city, chapel, flower, oak, atlantic, queen elizabeth.

2 Which of the following are **concrete nouns** and which are **abstract nouns**?

hat, sorrow, basket, folly, tyre, sadness, floor, mountain, grief, bliss, hut, ceiling, silence, lamp, faith, computer, gluttony, dish, rug, depression, contentment, dustbin, hatred, plum, sofa, clarity, portrait, finger, hospitality, tool, enmity.

3 Which of the following are **countable nouns** and which are **uncountable nouns**?

happiness, saucer, source, discretion, fence, lawn, misery, cooker, information, beach, location, luggage, bottle, forest, poem, inspiration, jewel, milk, suitcase, music, poetry, essay, literature, choir, legislation, beauty, cookery, knowledge.

4 Underline the words in the following sentences which are **verbal nouns**:

Walking is excellent exercise.
Smoking can kill you.

She hates dancing.
He has taken up running.
She enjoys swimming.

5 What is the **collective noun** for a group of the following?

wolves, cattle, flies, lions, stars, herring, geese, sheep, ships, whales.

6 Give the **plural** forms of the following words.

house, table, friend, dog, road, elephant, umbrella, banana, taxi, berry, bush, march, variety, kiss, lady, story, porch, child, loaf, wolf, tooth, woman.

7 Give the **singular** forms of the following words.

feet, geese, scarves, wives, halves, sheep, criteria, larvae, phenomena, bacteria, formulae, appendices.

8 Write down the words in the following list which are of **feminine** gender.

nephew, town, widow, empress, car, bridegroom, duchess, road, drake, sister, desk, niece, duke, waitress.

9 Write down the words in the following list that can be of **dual gender**.

artist, egg, writer, shoe, widower, king, poet, author, doctor, letter, princess, teacher, newspaper, bride, drake, parent, student, waitress, singer, athlete.

10 Give the **plural** forms of the following **compound nouns**.

passer-by, swimming pool, looker-on, coffee pot, show-off, police station, letter-box, cover-up.

11 Underline the phrase in each of the following sentences which is **in apposition** to a noun phrase.

The most important people involved, the pupils in the school, have not been consulted at all.
My favourite house, the one we saw last, is far too expensive for our budget.
Her cousin Mark, a senior partner in the firm, has just been arrested for fraud.
The local beach, a favourite meeting-place for teenagers, has been closed temporarily.

12 Write out those of the following sentences that contain a **personal pronoun** used as the **subject** of a sentence, underlining the relevant **personal pronoun**.

You must leave right away.
People simply don't trust you.
She didn't tell us what to do.
They nearly killed their victim.
You should have told the truth.
The police don't believe you.
He was driving dangerously.
Her colleagues admire her.
A bunch of flowers will make her feel better.

We gave them invitations to the wedding.

13 Write out the following sentences filling in the blanks with either **me** or **I**.

Jack asked ... to give you this.
Jane and ... are going on holiday together.
He is going to play chess against ....
Can Sue and ... come to the party?
Just ask for ... at the front desk.
There's been trouble between my neighbours and ...
The students and ... welcome this opportunity to put our point of view.
Just between you and ... I think he's a bit crazy.

14 Write out any of the sentences below that contain a **reflexive pronoun** used as an **emphatic pronoun**, underlining the relevant **emphatic pronouns**.

The children themselves should choose a book to be read aloud.
We hurt ourselves badly when falling off our skis.
We ourselves helped him as much as we could, but others did nothing.
Doctors think that he harmed himself deliberately.
You yourselves will have to do the bulk of the work.
The child cut herself with her mother's scissors.
The prime minister himself must take full responsibility for the error of judgement.
The house itself is not very attractive, but it has a beautiful garden.

15 Underline the words in the following sentences which are **demonstrative pronouns**.

This is not the ring which I lost.
Let me have a look at those.
That is an attractive plant.
These are the most expensive cars in the saleroom.
Those are the members of the jury.
This is the bus you must take.

16 Underline the words in the following sentences which are **indefinite pronouns**.

Nothing has been done to remedy the situation.
I didn't see anything which I wanted to buy.
Something must be seriously wrong.
I didn't recognize anyone in the crowd.
Nobody seems to know what happened.
Everyone was affected by the bad weather.

17 Underline the words in the following sentences which are **interrogative pronouns**.

Who made this mess?
Why change jobs now?
Whose is the briefcase on the chair?
Which do you like best?
How does he do it?
Where has he gone to?
Whose bike did you borrow?
To whom did he apply for the job?

18 Underline the words in the following sentences which are **relative pronouns**.

I think I know the man who did this.
There is the woman whose car was in the accident.
He doesn't know who she is.
Here is the book which won first prize.
He walked so slowly that he was late.
The flat that we liked best had already been sold.
Who got the job is not yet known.
This is the employee to whom the threatening letter was addressed.
It was her husband whom she blamed for the disaster.

19 Underline the **antecedent** in each of the following sentences.

Here are the keys which he lost.
That is the student who was accused of cheating.
The boy whose bike this is was injured in the accident.
The newspaper that first published the story got the facts wrong.
This is the address of the official to whom you should apply.

ANSWERS 3

1 proper nouns
Tuesday, October, Venus, America, Mount Everest, Uncle William, New York, Atlantic, Queen Elizabeth.

2 concrete nouns
hat, basket, tyre, floor, mountain, hut, ceiling, lamp, computer, dish, rug, dustbin, plum, sofa, portrait, finger, tool.

abstract nouns
sorrow, folly, sadness, grief, bliss, silence, faith, gluttony, depression, contentment, hatred, clarity, hospitality, enmity.

3 countable nouns
saucer, source, fence, lawn, cooker, beach, location, bottle, forest, poem, jewel, suitcase, essay, literature, choir.

uncountable nouns
happiness, discretion, misery, information, luggage, inspiration, milk, music, poetry, legislation, beauty, cookery, knowledge.

4 *Walking is excellent exercise.*
Smoking can kill you.
She hates dancing.
He has taken up running.
She enjoys swimming.

5 *a pack of wolves, a herd of cattle, a swarm of flies, a pride of lions, a constellation of stars, a shoal of herring, a flock of geese, a flock of sheep, a fleet of ships, a school of whales.*

6 *houses, tables, friends, dogs, roads, elephants, umbrellas, bananas, taxis, berries, bushes, marches, varieties,* *kisses, ladies, stories, porches, children, loaves, wolves, teeth, women.*

7 *foot, goose, scarf, wife, half, sheep, criterion, larva, phenomenon, bacterium, formula, appendix.*

8 *widow, empress, duchess, sister, niece, waitress.*

9 *artist, writer, poet, author, doctor, teacher, parent, student, singer, athlete.*

10 *passers-by, swimming pools, lookers-on, coffee pots, show-offs, police stations, letter-boxes, cover-ups.*

11 *The most important people involved, <u>the pupils in the school</u>, have not been consulted at all.*
My favourite house, <u>the one we saw last</u>, is far too expensive for our budget.
Her cousin Mark, <u>a senior partner in the firm</u>, has just been arrested for fraud.
The local beach, <u>a favourite meeting-place for teenagers</u>, has been closed temporarily.

12 *<u>You</u> must leave right away.*
<u>She</u> didn't tell us what to do.
<u>They</u> nearly killed their victim.
<u>You</u> should have told the truth.
<u>He</u> was driving dangerously.
<u>We</u> gave them invitations to the wedding.

13 *Jack asked **me** to give you this.*
*Jane and **I** are going on holiday together.*

*He is going to play chess against **me**.*
*Can Sue and **I** come to the party?*
*Just ask for **me** at the front desk.*
*There's been trouble between my neighbours and **me**.*
*The students and **I** welcome this opportunity to put our point of view.*
*Just between you and **me** I think he's a bit crazy.*

14 *The children <u>themselves</u> should choose a book to be read aloud.*
We <u>ourselves</u> helped him as much as we could, but others did nothing.
You <u>yourselves</u> will have to do the bulk of the work
The prime minister <u>himself</u> must take full responsibility for the error of judgement.
The house <u>itself</u> is not very attractive, but it has a beautiful garden.

15 *<u>This</u> is not the ring which I lost.*
Let me have a look at <u>those</u>.
<u>That</u> is an attractive plant.
<u>These</u> are the most expensive cars in the saleroom.
<u>Those</u> are the members of the jury.
<u>This</u> is the bus you must take.

16 *<u>Nothing</u> has been done to remedy the situation.*
I didn't see <u>anything</u> which I wanted to buy.
<u>Something</u> must be seriously wrong.
I didn't recognize <u>anyone</u> in the crowd.
<u>Nobody</u> seems to know what happened.

Everyone was affected by the bad weather.

17 *Who made this mess?*
Whose is the briefcase on the chair?
Which do you like best?
Whose did you borrow?
To whom did he apply for the job?

18 *I think I know the man who did this.*
There is the woman whose car was in the accident.
He doesn't know who she is.
Here is the book which won first prize.
He walked so slowly that he was late.
The flat that we liked best had already been sold.
Who got the job is not yet known.
This is the employee to whom the threatening letter was addressed.
It was her husband whom she blamed for the disaster.

19 *Here are the keys which he lost.*
That is the student who was accused of cheating.
The boy whose bike this is was injured in the accident.
The newspaper that first published the story got the facts wrong.
This is the address of the official to whom you should apply.

PARTS OF SPEECH II

Adjectives

An **adjective** is a word that describes or gives more information about nouns or pronouns.

An adjective is said to **qualify** a noun or pronoun because it limits the word it describes in some way by making it more specific. Thus, qualifying the word *book* with the adjective *red* means that we know that we are concentrating on a *red book* and that we can forget about books of any other colour. Similarly, qualifying the word *car* with the word *large* means that we know that we are concentrating on a *large car* and that we can forget about cars of another size. *See* **determiner**, page 141.

Adjectives usually tell us something about the colour, size, quantity, quality or classification of a noun or pronoun.

In the following sentences the underlined words are **adjectives**:

She wore a <u>white</u> dress.
It was a <u>tiny</u> dog.
They had <u>five</u> children.
They were <u>sad</u> people.
It was a <u>Victorian</u> house.

Gradable and non-gradable adjectives

Most adjectives are **gradable adjectives**. Such adjectives refer to qualities that can vary in degree. Such adjectives can take a **comparative** and a **superlative** (*see* pages 137, 139) form or can be accompanied by an **adverb of degree** such as *very*. Adjectives which do not take a comparative and superlative form and cannot be modified by an adverb of degree are called **non-gradable adjectives**.

In the following sentences the underlined words are **gradable adjectives**:

He drove a <u>small</u> car.
It was a <u>bright</u> shade of red.
We were <u>happy</u>.

In the following sentences the underlined words are **non-gradable adjectives**:

There was a <u>wooden</u> fence round the garden.
It was a <u>plastic</u> toy.
It was a <u>unique</u> experience.

Position of adjectives

Adjectives can be placed immediately before nouns or they can be joined to their relevant nouns by a verb. A few adjectives go directly after the noun. **Adjectives** are classified as follows in this respect.

Attributive adjectives

Attributive adjectives are placed immediately before the nouns which they qualify.

In the following sentences the underlined words are **attributive adjectives**:

The <u>blue</u> dress suited her very well.
They lived in a <u>huge</u> house.
We lived there for <u>six</u> years.
They sell delicious <u>cakes</u>.
They built a <u>wooden</u> hut in the garden.
They live in a <u>Georgian</u> square.

NB: Attributive position
Some **adjectives** are found only in the **attributive** position. The underlined words in the following list are examples of these:

my <u>former</u> boss
her <u>chief</u> reason for being here
his <u>sheer</u> folly in doing that
the <u>utter</u> beauty of the scene
paying <u>scant</u> attention to his work
in a <u>commanding</u> lead
the <u>searing</u> heat
a <u>thankless</u> task
a <u>fateful</u> meeting.

Predicative adjectives

Predicative adjectives are joined to their relevant nouns by a verb. They are so called because they help to form the **predicate** (*see* page 24) of a sentence.

The curtains in the bedroom were <u>blue</u>.
The dog was <u>huge</u>.
We were <u>hungry</u>.
The result is still <u>uncertain</u>.

Some **adjectives** are followed by a **preposition** such as *to, of* or *with*. In the following sentences the underlined words form a **predicative adjective** plus preposition:

The bug was <u>resistant to</u> the antibiotics.
She is <u>allergic to</u> eggs.
He is <u>afraid of</u> his boss.
The house is <u>devoid of</u> charm.
The behaviour is <u>characteristic of</u> a recovering alcoholic.
Is he <u>capable of</u> murder?
The task was <u>fraught with</u> danger.
A baby is just not <u>compatible with</u> such a lifestyle.
She is <u>reliant on</u> her parents.
She is <u>good at</u> tennis.

Post-modifiers

Adjectives which are **post-modifiers** go immediately after the noun which they qualify. In the following sentences the underlined words are **post-modifiers**:

The president-<u>elect</u> takes over the presidency at the beginning of the year.
The soldier is to appear before a court <u>martial</u>.

Qualitative adjectives

There are various types of adjective. The two main groups are **qualitative adjectives** and **classifying adjectives**. **Qualitative adjectives** tell you something about a quality that someone or someone has, as in:

sad, happy, wealthy, foolish, intelligent.

In the following sentences the underlined words are **qualitative adjectives:**

He is a <u>violent</u> man.
It was an <u>effective</u> remedy.
Please give a <u>brief</u> description.
You did some <u>useful</u> work.
They are <u>busy</u> people.
We had a <u>pleasant</u> day.
We have a <u>new</u> car.
It is a <u>huge</u> house.

NB: Qualitative adjectives include adjectives relating to size, such as *tiny* and *massive*.

Classifying adjectives

Classifying adjectives identify the particular class that something belongs to. For example, if you take the noun *pain*, there are various kinds or classes of pain such as *mental pain, physical pain* and *emotional pain*. The adjectives *mental, physical* and *emotional* are all examples of **classifying adjectives**. In the following sentences the underlined words are **classifying adjectives**:

It is not a <u>democratic</u> government.
They need a <u>financial</u> system.
The country has an <u>agricultural</u> economy.
This is not a <u>medical</u> problem.
This is an <u>urban</u> issue.
We have <u>annual</u> meetings.

Colour adjectives

Colour adjectives identify the colour of something, as in *black, red, yellow, purple* and *brown*.

In order to give a more precise description of a colour you can precede the colour adjective with a word such as *dark, pale, bright, light, deep*. The underlined words in the following sentences are examples of this:

She has <u>light brown</u> hair.
He wore a <u>dark blue</u> shirt.
It was a <u>bright green</u> hat.
She wants a <u>deep purple</u> dress.

If you wish to be less precise about the colour of something you can add the suffix *–ish* to the relevant colour, as in *greenish, yellowish*.

Number adjectives

See **number determiners**, page 147.

Emphatic adjectives

Emphatic adjectives are adjectives which you place in front of a noun to emphasise your feelings about something or to emphasise the degree of something, as in *absolute, pure*. In the following sentences the underlined words are **emphatic adjectives**:

The play was an <u>utter</u> disaster.
It was <u>pure</u> magic.
He is an <u>utter</u> idiot.
She is a <u>complete</u> fool.
The whole thing was a <u>positive</u> nightmare.
The campaign was a <u>total</u> failure.

Interrogative adjectives

The **adjectives** *which?* and *what?* are known as **interrogative adjectives**. They are used to ask questions about the nouns which they qualify. In the following sentences the underlined words are **interrogative adjectives**:

<u>Which</u> *book would you like to borrow?*
<u>Which</u> *bus goes to the centre of town?*
<u>What</u> *school did you go to?*
<u>What</u> *plans have you made for the wedding?*
<u>Which</u> *dress did you choose in the end?*
<u>What</u> *restaurant have they gone to?*

Demonstrative adjectives

Formerly **demonstrative determiners** were commonly known as **demonstrative adjectives**. *See* **determiners** and **demonstrative determiners** (pages 141, 145).

Possessive adjectives

Formerly **possessive determiners** were commonly known as **possessive adjectives**. *See* **determiners** and **possessive determiners** (pages 141, 146).

Compound adjectives

Compound adjectives are made up of two or more words, usually separated by a hyphen. In the following list the underlined words are **compound adjectives**:

a *grey-haired* man
a *part-time* post
a *black-and-white* cat
an *air-conditioned* office
a *kind-hearted* woman
a *good-looking* young woman
a *broken-hearted* young man
a *first-class* hotel.

Order of adjectives

If several **adjectives** are used to qualify a noun they tend to be placed in a certain order. The usual order is qualitative adjectives, such as *pretty*, adjectives relating to size, such as *large*, verb participles used as adjectives, such as *exciting, depressing, broken, disappointed, worried*, adjectives relating to colour, such as *orange*, adjectives relating to nationality or region, such as *American* or *northern*, adjectives relating to classification, such as *wooden, Victorian*, followed by adjectives relating to purpose or use such as *dining table*. The following sentences show the usual sequence of adjectives:

They live in a pretty little white house.
She wore a beautiful short black dress.
There was a large deep circular pond in the garden.
The roses were growing in the small enchanting Italian country garden.
They lived in an ugly depressing city suburb.
They sat round a large polished mahogany dining table.

NB: Order of adjectives
English is a very flexible language and the usual order of adjectives can be changed for emphasis.

Adjectives used as nouns

Sometimes adjectives can be used as **nouns**, especially when they are preceded by the definite article. In the following sentences the underlined words are adjectives used as nouns. It is sometimes considered offensive to use this construction, such as *the disabled,* as it can sound as though you are just lumping people together rather than considering them as individuals:

There are few opportunities for the <u>unemployed</u> around here.
The <u>poor</u> seem to keep getting poorer.
The <u>old</u> are often lonely.

Sometimes **colour adjectives** function as nouns without the definite or indefinite article:

<u>Yellow</u> is meant to make people feel more optimistic.
<u>Blue</u> is her favourite colour.
He always wears <u>black</u>.

NB: List commas
In cases where there is a list of adjectives before a noun, the use of commas between the adjectives is now optional although it was formerly standard practice. When the adjective immediately before the noun has a closer relationship with it than the other adjectives, and indeed often helps to define the noun, no comma should be used before that adjective, as

We want to buy some large juicy green peppers.

See **The comma as a separating device in a list of adjectives** on page 245.

Adjective or adverb?

Some words can be used both as **adjectives** and **adverbs**.

Which part of speech they are is obvious from the context in which they appear. The word *early* is an **adjective** in the first of the following sentences and an **adverb** in the second.

We caught the <u>early</u> train.
The train left <u>early</u> and we missed it.

Comparative forms of adjectives

Many adjectives have a **comparative form** used to indicate that something has more of a quality than something else. It is mostly qualitative adjectives that take comparative forms, although a few colour adjectives can also do so.

Some adjectives add *-er* to the absolute form to form their comparative form such as *braver* and *louder*. Some other adjectives are preceded by the word *more* to form their comparative form such as *more beautiful* and *more suitable*.

Which is the correct form of the comparative to use is often largely a matter of length. Adjectives which consist of one syllable, such as *loud,* usually add *-er* to make *louder*.

Comparative and number of syllables

When a one-syllable adjective ends in a single vowel followed by a single consonant, the consonant is doubled before the *-er* ending is added, as in *big, bigger.*

Some adjectives which consist of two syllables form their comparative by adding *-er*. This is especially true of adjectives which end in *-y*, such as *merry/merrier*, but it is also true of some other two-syllable adjectives such as *clever/ cleverer* and *quiet/quieter*. In other cases, such as *famous* or *careful*, the comparative form is formed with *more*, as in *more famous, more careful*. In some cases the comparative of a two-syllable adjective can be formed either by adding *-er* to the positive or absolute form or by preceding this with *more*. Thus the word *gentle* can have the comparative form *gentler* or *more gentle* and the word *pleasant* can have the comparative form *pleasanter* or *more pleasant*.

Adjectives which consist of three or more syllables usually have comparative forms using *more*, such as *more dangerous*. Some three-syllable adjectives which begin with the prefix *-un* can form their comparative forms by adding *-er* , such as *unhappy/unhappier, unlucky/unluckier*.

The above are regular ways of forming the comparative of adjectives. In the following sentences the underlined words are examples of these:

She is prettier than her sister.
It was a brighter day.
The walls are whiter now.
He is younger than his wife.
It's a safer place now.
The house is even dirtier.
It's a heavier burden.
She is the more careful worker.
He was the cleverer student.

She is <u>madder</u> than ever.
That death was <u>sadder</u> still.
The child is <u>quieter</u> than her brother.
He is the <u>more honest</u> of the two business partners.
I chose the <u>bigger</u> room.
She gets <u>lovelier</u> each year.
This is an even <u>riskier</u> venture.
This essay is far <u>more interesting</u>.
This doorway is <u>narrower</u> than the other.
This is a <u>politer/more polite</u> way of saying the same thing.
This is certainly a <u>pleasanter/more pleasant</u> way of spending the day.
That is the <u>likelier/more likely</u> solution.
That is an even <u>more ridiculous</u> idea.

Irregular comparatives

The adjectives *good* and *bad* have the irregular comparative forms *better* and *worse*, as in *a good day/a better day* and *a bad experience/a worse experience*.

No comparative form

Some adjectives have only an absolute form and do not normally have a comparative form. These include *mere, perfect, real, right, unique* and *utter*.

Superlative forms

You can also describe something by saying that something has more of a quality than anything else of its kind. In order to do this you use the **superlative form** of an adjective. The regular superlative form of an adjective is formed in the same way as the comparative form, except that the comparative ending *-er* is replaced by the superlative ending *-est,* and the word *more*, which is used to form the comparative, is replaced by the word *most*. Thus, in the following sentences the underlined words are examples of the superlative form of adjectives:

I want the <u>largest</u> size.
It was the <u>longest</u> journey I've ever taken.
That is the <u>maddest</u> idea yet.
He is the <u>unhappiest</u> person I know.
It was the <u>most disappointing</u> news that I had had all year.
This is the <u>quietest</u> room in the hotel.
He is certainly the <u>cleverest</u> student.
She was the <u>most beautiful</u> woman there.
The rose is the <u>loveliest</u> flower.
This seems the <u>most dangerous</u> plan.

Irregular superlatives

The adjectives *good* and *bad* have the irregular superlative forms *best* and *worst,* as in *a good day/the best day* and *a bad experience/the worst experience.*

No superlative form

Some adjectives have only an absolute form and do not normally have a superlative form. These include *mere, perfect, real, right, unique* and *utter.*

Determiners

A **determiner** is a word that is used in front of a noun or pronoun to give some information about it. Formerly, **determiners** were classified as **adjectives**. However, because, unlike adjectives, determiners do not, strictly speaking 'describe' a noun or pronoun, the modern grammatical practice is to draw a distinction between them. Thus, the category **determiner** has been created.

Types of determiner

Definite and indefinite articles

The **definite and indefinite articles** are often categorized as **determiners**.

Definite article

The **definite article** is *the* and it can be used in various ways. It can be used in a sentence to refer back to a person or thing that has already been mentioned or identified.

In the following sentences *the* is used in this way:

Mrs Brown gave birth to a boy and the boy was called John.
I was asked to choose a restaurant and the restaurant I chose was The Olive Tree.
Father bought a new dog and the dog is a Labrador.

The **definite article** can also be used to identify someone or something as the only one of its kind. In the following sentences *the* is used in this way:

He is reading <u>the</u> Bible.
Tourists often visit <u>the</u> Tower of London.
He has been declared <u>the</u> new Prime Minister of the UK.

The **definite article** is used to refer to a whole class or group of things or people. In the following sentences *the* is used in this way:

Lions belong to <u>the</u> big cats.
She really does not like <u>the</u> English.
Because of a long-lasting family feud <u>the</u> Smiths did not speak to the Simpsons at John and Jane's wedding.

Less commonly, the **definite article** can be used to indicate the unique quality of someone or something. In this context *the* is emphasized and is pronounced *thee*. In the following sentences *the* is used in this way:

In the sixties it was <u>the</u> restaurant to go to in London.
It is currently <u>the</u> city venue for fashionable wedding receptions.
The musical is <u>the</u> show to see this Christmas.

Indefinite article

The form of the **indefinite article** is either *a* or *an*. The form *a* is used before words that begin with a consonant sound such as *a box, a garden, a road, a star, a wall*. The form *an* is used before words that begin with an initial vowel sound such as *an apple, an egg, an igloo, an ostrich, an uncle*.

> **NB: It's the sound that counts**
> It is the <u>sound</u> of the initial letter and not the spelling that counts in this case. Thus, *a* is used before words beginning with the letter *u* when these are pronounced as though they began with the consonant *y*, as *a unit*. Similarly, *an* is used before words beginning with the letter *h* where this is not pronounced, as *an heir, an hour, an honest man*.
>
> Formerly it was quite common to use *an* before words which begin with the *h* sound and also begin with an unstressed syllable, as *an hotel, an historic occasion, an habitual criminal* and *an hereditary disease*. Nowadays, it is more usual to use *a* in these cases, as in *a hotel, a historic occasion, a habitual criminal, a hereditary disease*.

The **indefinite article** can also be used in various ways. It can be used in the same way as the adjective *one*. In the following sentences *a/an* is used in this way:

The town is exactly a mile away.
We waited an hour for the bus to come.
A year ago we were happy, but things have changed.

NB: Just the one
If you wish to stress that you are referring to just *one* of something, rather than to several, you use the pronunciation *ay* to rhyme with *hay*, as in:

I wanted a (ay) biscuit, not a packet of them.
It's OK to have a (ay) drink, but you will certainly not be fit to drive if you have half a bottle of wine.

The **indefinite article** is also used to refer to or single out a specific person or thing. In the following sentences *a/an* is used in this way:
Jim married a girl called Mary from the next village.
The family had a black cat called Sooty.
Sue is going out with a young man called Tom.

The **indefinite article** is also used with an indefinite meaning, in the same way that *any* is. In the following sentence *a/an* is used in this way:
He was as big as a house.
An island is a piece of land entirely surrounded by water.
A paediatrician is a doctor who specializes in children's illnesses.

The **indefinite article** is also used in the following way, with the word 'for' implied but omitted before it:
The grapes are £3 a kilo.
The gardener will charge you £12 an hour.
The cake is £2 a slice.

NB: Zero article
The absence of both the definite or indefinite articles is sometimes referred to as **zero article**. The following sentences contain examples of this:

We went by train.
He is in hospital.
Have you had lunch?
She's at work.

Demonstrative determiners

Formerly known as **demonstrative adjectives, demonstrative determiners** are used to point out or indicate the nouns which they qualify.

The **demonstrative determiners** are *this, that, these* and *those*, as in *this book, that house, these flowers* and *those girls*.

In the following sentences the underlined words are examples of **demonstrative determiners**:

This cake is absolutely delicious.
I do admire those flowers.
I used to live in that house.
These students are all taking the exam.
I love this dress, but I can't afford it.
Who is that man over there?
Why are those people laughing at us?
These trees are huge.
Those red grapes are delicious.
These green grapes are sour.

Possessive determiners

When you wish to indicate that something belongs to someone or something or that it is connected in some way with someone or something you use the **possessive determiners** *my, our, your, his/her/its, their*. Formerly, **possessive determiners** were commonly known as **possessive adjectives**. In the following sentences the underlined words are **possessive determiners**:

I would like my book back, please.
Where are your children?
Dad let me borrow his car.
He was brushing his teeth.
She looks very like her mother.
Unfortunately, the dog broke its leg in the accident.
The children loved their new bikes.

(*See* **possessive pronouns** under **personal pronouns**, page 110.)

Indefinite determiners

The **indefinite determiners**, also called **general determiners**, are used to qualify nouns or pronouns when you are talking about people or things in a general or indefinite way, without identifying them.

The **indefinite** or **general determiners** include *all, any, both, each, either, every, few, little, less, many, much, more, neither, no, several, some and neither*, as underlined in the following sentences:

Any room in the hotel will do.
Both students are to blame.
Neither house is really suitable.
Either bus will take you to the village.
Every car has been damaged.
Many books were destroyed in the fire.
Few patients have survived such an operation.
No facts are known yet.
Some gardens are beautifully kept.
Several buses go into the centre of town.
Little information has been released.
We have enough children to start a new class.
He does not have enough knowledge.
He has no more work.
There have been more accidents on that stretch of road.
Are there any jobs available?

Number determiners

Numbers when they are used before a noun are sometimes classified as **determiners**, and sometimes as **adjectives**. Numbers such as *one, two, ten, twenty*, etc are called **cardinal numbers**, while numbers such as *first, second, tenth, twentieth*, etc are called **ordinal numbers**.

In the following sentences the underlined words are **cardinal numbers**:

We only have one chance to succeed.
There are seven people in the house.

More than <u>sixty</u> soldiers died in the battle.
There are <u>five hundred and fifty</u> pupils in the school.

In the following sentences the underlined words are **ordinal numbers**:

This is the <u>third</u> time he's been in prison.
This is the little girl's <u>fourth</u> birthday.
They're celebrating their <u>twenty-fifth</u> wedding anniversary.

EXERCISES 4

1 Which of the underlined adjectives in the following sentences are **attributive** and which are **predicative**?

It was a <u>delightful</u> trip.
The bride was <u>beautiful</u>.
She has an <u>interesting</u> job.
The job was <u>boring.</u>
The meal was <u>delicious</u>.
The basket was full of <u>ripe</u> fruit.
The dog was safely behind <u>iron</u> gates.
The <u>hungry</u> children ate all the food quickly.
They aren't <u>busy</u> today.
The <u>violent</u> man was arrested by the police.
The weather was very <u>pleasant</u>.
The carpet was <u>red</u>.
The <u>difficult</u> task took a long time.
The <u>white</u> dress stained very easily.
She combed her <u>long</u> hair.
Her eyes were <u>brown</u>.
They do a <u>useful</u> job.
The story was <u>brief</u>.
The <u>new</u> car was expensive.
The child was <u>sad</u>.

2 Write out the following sentences replacing the blanks with the appropriate **prepositions**.

There was a garden, but it was devoid ... flowers.
He is not at all good ... administration.
Do you think they are capable ... such deceit?
Some people are naturally resistant ... the disease.
The child is allergic ... dairy products.
His symptoms are characteristic ... a neurological disorder.
Such investments are fraught ... risk.

3 Write out the sentences which contain an **emphatic adjective**, underlining the **emphatic adjectives**.

She is an absolute idiot to trust that man.
She gave the right answer.
The whole evening was a total success.
It was a true story.
The end-of-school play was a positive triumph for the drama department.
She gave a positive response to his queries.
The situation was a complete disaster.
The prince requires his bride to be virtuous and pure.
He must be an utter maniac to do such a thing.

4 Write out those of the following sentences which contain an **adjective**, underlining the **adjectives**.

He ran fast, but failed to win the race.
The early flight leaves at 7 a.m.

If you arrive late you will not be allowed into the concert.
It was a fast race and several of the runners did not finish.
There's a late bus that leaves at midnight.
We got there early for our appointment.

5 Write out the following sentences, inserting in each blank the **comparative** form of the adjective given in bold in brackets.

She is ... than ever. (lovely)
The streets here are much ... than they are in other areas of the town. (dirty)
This week's lecture was ... than last week's. (interesting)
Her story is even ... than that of the other orphans. (sad)
They are ... now than they have ever been. (unhappy)
You must be ... when walking in that area. (careful).
He seems to be the ... of the two brothers. (honest)
This load seems to get ... the further I walk. (heavy)
The writer is over-shadowed by his ... brother. (famous)
The place is ... now since the students moved out. (quiet)

6 Write out the following sentences, inserting in each blank the **superlative** form of the adjective given in bold in brackets.
This is the ... result that we could have had. (disappointing)
The teenager had the ... birthday of her life (good)
It is the ... village on that coast. (beautiful)
It was the ... experience of my life. (bad)

She was the ... woman at the ball. **(lovely)**
This is the ... day of the year. **(long)**
That was the ... period of his entire life. **(unhappy)**

7 Write out the following sentences, inserting the correct form of the **indefinite article** in the blanks.

He lives ... mile away from the city centre.
The fee will be £15 ... hour.
They're building ... wall round the back garden.
The child was eating ... apple.
We packed up all the books in ... box.
The house has no heating and it's like ... igloo.
We need ... star for the top of the Christmas tree.
She's like ... ostrich that's burying its head in the sand.
He has ... hereditary heart disease that is likely to shorten his life.
The metre is ... unit of length.

8 Write out the sentences which contain **ordinal numbers** and underline these numbers.

They have six children.
Jack is her second husband.
The businessman owns three local companies.
The baby is their first grandchild.
There were five members of the gang.
This is your third, and final, warning.
There is only one thing to be done.

They're having a party to celebrate their twenty-fifth wedding anniversary.
Sue is their seventh child.
We need at least twenty workers to finish the job in time.
They've been on four holidays this year.
He is celebrating his ninetieth birthday.
This is the third cold I've had this winter.

9 Write out the sentences which contain **indefinite determiners** and underline these determiners.

That man looks ill.
He owns this house.
Several trains have been cancelled today.
Few victims recovered.
Her dog attacked my cat.
Less help was given to pensioners this year.
The monkey broke out of its cage.
These paintings are lovely.
Both men were charged with the offence.
Is this your coat?
Neither jacket is mine.
Every bag must be searched.
There is no room in the hall for all these people.
We do not have enough information on which to act.
Dad took his car to work.
This is a complete disaster.
Why blame this error on me?
Some children will have to go to the school in the city.

10 Write out the sentences which contain **possessive determiners** and underline these determiners.

You lied to me.
This book is mine, not yours.
He parked his car in the next street.
She took her children with her.
Jack and Sue have left their flat empty for the whole summer.
We must get back there before nightfall.
I think this note book is yours.
Our rose garden is lovely at this time of year.
They need to take action right away.
Their assistance is required.
Your experience will be invaluable.
His attitude to his work annoys his colleagues.
Her neglect of her children is absolutely shameful.

ANSWERS 4

1 **attributive adjectives** *delightful, interesting, ripe, iron, hungry, violent, difficult, white, long, useful, new.*
predicative adjectives *beautiful, boring, delicious, busy, pleasant, red, brown, brief, sad.*

2 *There was a garden, but it was devoid **of** flowers.*
*He is not at all good **at** administration.*
*Do you think they are capable **of** such deceit?*
*Some people are naturally resistant **to** the disease.*
*The child is allergic **to** dairy products.*
*His symptoms are characteristic **of** a neurological disorder.*
*Such investments are fraught **with** risk.*

3 *She is an <u>absolute</u> idiot to trust that man.*
The whole evening was a <u>total</u> success.
The end-of-school play was a <u>positive</u> triumph for the drama department.
The situation was a <u>complete</u> disaster.
He must be an <u>utter</u> maniac to do such a thing.

4 *The <u>early</u> flight leaves at 7 a.m.*
It was a <u>fast</u> race and several of the runners did not finish.
There's a <u>late</u> bus that leaves at midnight.

5 *She is **lovelier** than ever.*

*The streets here are much **dirtier** than they are in other areas of the town.*

*This week's lecture was **more interesting** than last week's.*

*Her story is even **sadder** than that of the other orphans.*

*They are **unhappier** now than they have ever been.*

*You must be **more careful** when walking in that area.*

*He seems to be the **more honest** of the two brothers.*

*This load seems to get **heavier** the further I walk.*

*The writer is over-shadowed by his **more famous** brother.*

*The place is **quieter** now since the students moved out.*

6 *This is the **most disappointing** result that we could have had.*

*The teenager had the **best** birthday of her life.*

*It is the **most beautiful** village on that coast.*

*It was the **worst** experience of my life.*

*She was the **loveliest** woman at the ball.*

*This is the **longest** day of the year.*

*That was the **unhappiest** period of his entire life.*

7 *He lives **a** mile away from the city centre.*

*The fee will be £15 **an** hour.*

*They're building **a** wall round the back garden.*

*The child was eating **an** apple.*

*We packed up all the books in **a** box.*

*The house has no heating and it's like **an** igloo.*
*We need **a** star for the top of the Christmas tree.*
*She's like **an** ostrich that's burying its head in the sand.*
*He has **a** hereditary heart disease that is likely to shorten his life.*
*The metre is **a** unit of length.*

8 *Jack is her <u>second</u> husband.*
The baby is their <u>first</u> grandchild.
This is your <u>third,</u> and final, warning.
They're having a party to celebrate their <u>twenty-fifth</u> wedding anniversary.
Sue is their <u>seventh</u> child.
He is celebrating his ninetieth birthday.
This is the third cold I've had this winter.

9 *<u>Several</u> trains have been cancelled today.*
<u>Few</u> victims recovered.
<u>Less</u> help was given to pensioners this year.
<u>Both</u> men were charged with the offence.
<u>Neither</u> jacket is mine.
<u>Every</u> bag must be searched.
There is <u>no</u> room in the hall for all these people.
We do not have <u>enough</u> information on which to act.
<u>Some</u> children will have to go to the school in the city.

10 *He parked <u>his</u> car in the next street.*
She took <u>her</u> children with her.

Jack and Sue have left their flat empty for the whole summer.

Our rose garden is lovely at this time of year.

Their assistance is required.

Your experience will be invaluable.

His attitude to his work annoys his colleagues.

Her neglect of her children is absolutely shameful.

PARTS OF SPEECH III

Verbs

In simple terms the **verb** is known as a 'doing word'—you might have been told this in primary school. In many ways this description is an oversimplification and unduly restrictive since it tends to overlook the fact that, although many verbs do express action, many simply indicate a condition or state. The description also excludes **auxiliary verbs, modal verbs**, etc.

Nevertheless, the verb is usually the word in a sentence that is most concerned with the action and it is usually essential to the structure of a sentence. The verb is usually the most important part of the **predicate** (*see* page 27).

Verbs have a number of functions. In particular, they indicate **tense**, **voice**, **mood**, **number** and **person**.

Verbs are classified as **regular verbs** and **irregular verbs**.

Regular verbs

Most verbs are **regular verbs**, occasionally known as **weak verbs**. They are described as regular because they obey certain rules, especially regarding the forming of **tenses**. **Regular verbs** obey the following such rules:

1 Regular verbs add the ending *-s* to the base or infinitive form of the verb, as in *walk*, *play* and *look*, to form the **third person singular** of the **present tense**, as in:

he walks, *it plays*, *she looks*.

While the rest of the present tense is formed by using just the base or infinitive form, as in:

I walk, *you play*, *they look*.

The **present participle** of regular verbs is formed by adding the ending *-ing* to the base form, as in

walking, *playing*, *looking*.

If the base form ends in *-e* the *e* is usually omitted before the *-ing* ending is added, as in:

hating, *loving*, *loathing*.

2 Regular verbs add the ending *-ed* to the base (or the ending *-d* if the base form already ends in *-e*) to form the **past tense**.

This applies to all **persons**, as in:

I walked
they played
you killed
he worked
she loved
they hated.

In the following sentences the underlined words all form examples of **regular verbs**:

You rarely <u>smile</u>.
She <u>walked</u> slowly.
You all <u>seemed</u> so sad.
We <u>laugh</u> a lot.
They <u>look</u> happy.
He <u>plays</u> tennis.
She <u>reads</u> crime fiction.
She <u>is looking</u> pale.
<u>Loving</u> her as he did, he was distraught at her death.
It <u>rains</u> every day.
She <u>loathed</u> her boss.
He <u>looked</u> at the view from the window.

Irregular verbs

Irregular verbs do not obey the rules which apply to **regular verbs**. In particular, they deviate from the pattern of adding *-ed* or *-d* to the infinitive form to form the past tense and past participle forms.

Categories of irregular verbs

Irregular verbs fall into several categories when it comes to forming the past tense and past participle forms.

1 One category concerns those verbs which have the same form as the infinitive form in the past tense and past participle forms, as in:

to <u>cut</u>:
I <u>cut</u> my hand yesterday.
I have <u>cut</u> myself.

to <u>burst</u>:
The river <u>burst</u> its banks.
The child has <u>burst</u> the balloon.

The following verbs are included in this category:

infinitive	past tense	past participle
bet	bet	bet
burst	burst	burst
cast	cast	cast
cost	cost	cost
cut	cut	cut

infinitive	past tense	past participle
hit	hit	hit
hurt	hurt	hurt
put	put	put
set	set	set
shut	shut	shut
split	split	split
spread	spread	spread

2 Another category includes those **irregular verbs** which have two past tenses and two past participles, the past tenses having the same forms as the past participles, such as *spoil, spoiled/spoilt, have spoiled/spoilt*. The following verbs are included in this category:

infinitive	past tense	past participle
burn	burned/burnt	burned/burnt
dream	dreamed/dreamt	dreamed/dreamt
dwell	dwelled/dwelt	dwelled/dwelt
hang	hanged/hung	hanged/hung
kneel	kneeled/knelt	kneeled/knelt
lean	leaned/leant	leaned/leant
leap	leaped/leapt	leaped/leapt
learn	learned/learnt	learned/learnt
light	lighted/lit	lighted/lit
smell	smelled/smelt	smelled/smelt
speed	speeded/sped	speeded/sped
spill	spilled/spilt	spilled/spilt
spoil	spoiled/spoilt	spoiled/spoilt
weave	weaved/woven	weaved/woven
wet	wetted/wet	wetted/wet

3 Another category includes those **irregular verbs** which have past tenses that never end in -*ed* and which have the same form as that of the past participles. The following verbs are included in this category:

infinitive	past tense	past participle
bend	bent	bent
build	built	built
dig	dug	dug
feel	felt	felt
fight	fought	fought
find	found	found
get	got	got
hear	heard	heard
hold	held	held
keep	kept	kept
lay	laid	laid
lead	led	led
leave	left	left
lend	lent	lent
lose	lost	lost
make	made	made
mean	meant	meant
meet	met	met
pay	paid	paid
say	said	said
sell	sold	sold
send	sent	sent
shine	shone	shone
sit	sat	sat
sleep	slept	slept

infinitive	past tense	past participle
spend	spent	spent
stand	stood	stood
stick	stuck	stuck
strike	struck	struck
swing	swung	swung
teach	taught	taught
tell	told	told
think	thought	thought
understand	understood	understood
weep	wept	wept
win	won	won

4 Another category includes **irregular verbs** which have regular past tense forms ending in *-ed* or *-d* and two possible past participles, one of which is regular and the same as the past tense. The following verbs are included in this category:

infinitive	past tense	past participle
mow	mowed	mowed/mown
prove	proved	proved/proven
sew	sewed	sewed/sewn
show	showed	showed/shown
sow	sowed	sowed/sown
swell	swelled	swelled/swollen

5 Another category includes **irregular verbs** which have past tenses and past participles which are different from each other and different from the infinitive. Some common verbs in this category are included in the following list:

infinitive	past tense	past participle
bear	bore	borne
begin	began	begun
bite	bit	bitten
blow	blown	blew
break	broke	broken
choose	chose	chosen
do	did	done
draw	drew	drawn
drink	drank	drunk
drive	drove	driven
eat	ate	eaten
fall	fell	fallen
fly	flew	flown
forbid	forbade	forbidden
forgive	forgave	forgiven
forget	forgot	forgotten
freeze	froze	frozen
give	gave	given
grow	grew	grown
hide	hid	hidden
know	knew	known
lie	lay	lain
ride	rode	ridden
rise	rose	risen
ring	rang	rung
see	saw	seen
shake	shook	shaken
shrink	shrank	shrunk
speak	spoke	spoken
steal	stole	stolen

infinitive	past tense	past participle
swear	swore	sworn
swim	swam	swum
take	took	taken
tear	tore	torn
throw	threw	thrown
wake	woke	woken
wear	wore	worn
write	wrote	written

Tense

One of the most important functions of the verb is to indicate the time at which an action takes place, whether someone or something <u>is doing</u> something, <u>was doing</u> something or <u>will do</u> something. This is expressed by **tense** and in many languages this is marked by inflection.

In English, tense is marked by inflection only in the **present tense** and the **past tense**. Thus, in the case of the verb to *walk* the third person singular masculine of the present tense is *he walks* and the third person singular masculine of the past tense is *he walked*.

There are several tenses in English. The major ones are **present tense, past tense** and **future test**, but there are other categories relating to these.

Present tense

The **present tense** indicates an action now going on or a state now existing. It uses the base form, also known as the infinitive form, of the verb, as *walk, run, make, go* but it changes in the third person singular when it adds -*s* to the base form, sometimes with a spelling change, as *walks, runs, makes, goes*.

There are two forms of the present tense, the **simple present tense** and the **continuous present tense**.

Simple present tense

The **simple present tense** is used to indicate an action that is currently going on. In the following sentences the underlined words are all verbs in the **simple present tense**:

He <u>works</u> in the city.
She <u>lives</u> by the sea.
I <u>want</u> some food.
My head <u>hurts</u>.
He <u>is</u> an excellent chef.

The **simple present tense** is also used to indicate something that is always or generally true. In the following sentences the underlined words are all verbs in the **simple present tense**:

The world <u>is</u> round.
Three and three <u>make</u> six.
Thin glass <u>breaks</u> easily.
Tigers <u>are</u> carnivorous.
Milk <u>goes</u> sour quickly in heat.

The **simple present tense** is also used to indicate an action that is regular or habitual. In the following sentences the underlined words are verbs in the **simple present tense**:

I <u>rise</u> at seven.
He <u>drinks</u> whisky.

I <u>work</u> on Saturdays.
He <u>drives</u> a white van.
They <u>walk</u> to work.

The **simple present tense** is also used with some **adverbs** or **adverbials** of time to refer to a time in the future. In the following sentences the underlined words are verbs in the **simple present tense** referring to the future:

We <u>arrive</u> at midnight.
They <u>leave</u> early.
The holidays <u>start</u> tomorrow.
I <u>move</u> next month.
The match <u>begins</u> in an hour.

Continuous present tense

The **continuous present tense**, also called the **progressive present tense**, is used when you are talking about something that is happening at the very moment when you are speaking or when you are referring to an action continuing over a period of time, including the present, and not complete at the time when you are referring to it.

This tense is formed using the present tense of the verb *to be*, *is* and *are*, and the **present participle**, ending in *-ing* (*see* page 198) of the main verb. It frequently occurs in a **contracted form**, such as *I'm* for *I am, you're* for *you are, aren't* for *are not* etc.

In the following sentences the underlined words are verbs in the **continuous present tense**:

We are having a picnic.
I am studying the report.
She is feeling very nervous.
They are laughing loudly.
I'm driving home.
They aren't trying.
We're climbing the hill.
She's spending Christmas here.
The standard of work is improving.
The child is developing normally.
We are staying in a hotel in the centre of town.
I believe you are studying English at the local university.

The **continuous present tense** is also used with some **adverbs** or **adverbials** of time to refer to a time in the future. In the following sentences the underlined words are verbs in the **continuous present tense**:

We are having a meeting next week.
He's leaving next month.
I'm travelling tomorrow.
She's graduating next summer.

Past tense

The **past tense** refers to an action that has taken place before the present time. In the case of **regular verbs** (*see* page 160) it is formed by adding *-ed* to the base or infinitive form of the verb, as *walked, looked, started, failed*. For the **past tense** of **irregular verbs** *see* page 162.

There are two forms of the past tense, the **simple past tense** and the **continuous past tense**.

Simple past tense

The **simple past tense** is used to refer to an event or state that occurred at some point in the past. In the following sentences the underlined words are verbs in the past tense:

The car <u>crashed</u> into the van.
I <u>cracked</u> the vase.
The child <u>climbed</u> the tree.
The mother <u>rocked</u> the cradle.
She <u>loved</u> him very much.
They <u>hated</u> each other.
She <u>drowned</u> in the river.
They <u>drew</u> their swords.
We <u>slept</u> on the beach.
She <u>chose</u> a simple wedding dress.
He <u>stole</u> a car.
I <u>heard</u> a strange noise.
In time she <u>forgave</u> him.
The dog <u>stood</u> by the gate.
The bells <u>rang</u> out.
He <u>swore</u> that he would be faithful.
It <u>made</u> a huge difference to their lifestyle.

The **simple past tense** is also used to indicate a regular or repeated action in the past, as in:

They <u>worked</u> night shift.
The children <u>attended</u> the local primary school.
The policeman <u>walked</u> the beat nightly.
When I was a child we <u>lived</u> in the city.
People <u>drank</u> very little alcohol in those days.
The sun always <u>shone</u> when we were there.
As children we <u>rode</u> our ponies in the lanes around the village.

Continuous past tense

The **continuous past tense**, also called the **progressive past tense** and the **imperfect tense**, is used to refer to a continuing action that happened in the past and is probably now complete. This tense is formed by using the past tense of the verb *to be*, *was* and *were*, and the present participle, ending in *-ing*, of the main verb, as in:

We <u>were living</u> in the area at the time.

In the following sentences the words underlined form the **continuous past tense** of a verb:

We <u>were studying</u> at university then.
You <u>were building</u> your house that year.
They <u>were painting</u> the kitchen yesterday.
He <u>was running</u> in the marathon last week.
She <u>was serving</u> in the bar last night.
I <u>was sewing</u> the dress until midnight.

The **continuous past** is also used to refer to an event in the past that occurred during the course of another event. In the following sentences the words underlined are used to form the **continuous past tense** of the verb:

They <u>were walking</u> to the shops when they saw her across the road.
I <u>was running</u> down the hill when I tripped and fell.
You <u>were risking</u> your lives when you did that.
We <u>were driving</u> home when the car broke down.

Perfect tense

The **present perfect tense**, also known as the **perfect tense**, is another tense which refers to the past. It is formed using the **present tense** of the verb *have* and the **past participle** of the main verb (*see* page 199 and **irregular verbs**, page 162), as in:

I <u>have looked</u> everywhere for it.

It is used to refer to an action that began in the past but continues into the present time or to refer to an action in the past which has results continuing to the present. In the following sentences the underlined words form the **present perfect tense**:

He <u>has lived</u> in France for over thirty years.
Floods <u>have destroyed</u> thousands of books in the ware-house.
I <u>have made</u> your favourite dessert.
You <u>have ruined</u> this carpet by spilling wine on it.

It <u>has lasted</u> well, but now needs replaced.
We <u>have thought</u> a great deal about this.
They <u>have travelled</u> throughout Britain.
Age <u>has changed</u> him rather a lot.

Continuous present perfect tense

The **present perfect tense** also exists in a continuous or progressive form indicating an action in the past that is still going on. In the following sentences the underlined words are examples of the **continuous present perfect tense**:

I <u>have been living</u> abroad for many years now.
We <u>have been thinking</u> of buying a new house.
They <u>have been studying</u> the results carefully.
Our projects <u>have been developing</u> quite slowly because of lack of funding.
You <u>have been staring</u> out of the window for hours.

Past perfect tense

The **past perfect tense**, also known as **the pluperfect tense**, also refers to the past. It is formed using the **past tense** of the verb *have* and the **past participle** of the main verb (*see* page 199 and **irregular verbs** page 162), as in:

We <u>had discussed</u> the matter in detail.

The past perfect tense is used to refer to a past action that took place at an earlier time than another action, there sometimes being a causal link between the events, as in:

She went round to see him after she <u>had received</u> his message.

It is also used to refer to an action that continues right up to, or relates to, a single point in the past, as in:

By the end of the year the project <u>had been abandoned</u>.

In the following sentences the underlined words form examples of the **past perfect tense**:

By evening it was obvious that he <u>had decided</u> not to come.
His condition <u>had deteriorated</u> since I last saw him.
We <u>had known</u> each other for several years before we became partners.
By then we <u>had climbed</u> to the summit.
I <u>had expected</u> to see him there.
She <u>had resigned</u> from her job and was unemployed.

The **past perfect tense** also exists in a continuous or progressive form. In the following sentences the underlined words are examples of the **continuous past perfect tense**:

We <u>had been working</u> on the project for three months by then.
They <u>had been hoping</u> that we would fail.
It was clear that she <u>had been contemplating</u> leaving.
You <u>had</u> obviously <u>been thinking</u> of emigrating, although you did not.

Future tense

The **future tense** describes an action or state that will occur at some point in the future. The future tense is formed by using *will* or *shall* with the infinitive form of the main verb. It is used to predict or say what is likely to happen in the future, as in:

Work will begin next week.

Traditional grammar

According to traditional grammar rules *shall* should be used with *I* and *we*, and *will* should be used with *you, he/she/it* and *they,* as in:

We <u>shall</u> arrive in time for tea.
I <u>shall</u> take the bus to work today.
You <u>will</u> find fresh milk in the fridge.
He <u>will</u> give you the book tomorrow.
She <u>will</u> act as a temporary secretary.
It <u>will</u> certainly spoil things.
They <u>will</u> be punished for this.

Again, according to traditional rules, this order is reversed for emphasis and *will* is then used with *I* and *we*, as in:

I <u>will</u> succeed at this, believe me.
We <u>will</u> have the house of our dreams one day.
You <u>shall</u> get the dress you want if I have anything to do with it.

He <u>shall</u> be punished for this, if there's any justice.
My daughter <u>shall</u> have the wedding she dreams of.
They <u>shall</u> be made to pay for this, I assure you.

Modern usage

In modern usage things have changed and, increasingly, *will* is the preferred form in most modern contexts, whether these be spoken or written contexts, in all but the most formal. The only exception to this is the use of *shall* as used with *I* and *we* when questions are being asked, and, even then, this is a fairly formal context, as in:

Shall we proceed?
Shall I go on?
Shall we postpone the meeting until next week?
Shall I reserve a room for you?

In the following sentences the underlined words are used to form the future tense as it is found in modern usage:

I <u>will</u> have to leave now.
We <u>will</u> get the next bus.
You <u>will</u> require to give references.
He <u>will</u> see you now.
She <u>will</u> be back tomorrow.
It <u>will</u> take a miracle.
They <u>will</u> do anything you want.
<u>Shall</u> I send you an application form?
<u>Shall</u> we meet at the same time tomorrow?

Other ways of referring to the future

You can also use *be about to* or *be going to* with the infinitive form of the main verb to refer to the future. In the following sentences the underlined words refer to the future:

I <u>am going to see</u> her today.
You <u>are about to discover</u> what happened.
They <u>are going to experience</u> danger.
Things <u>are about to improve</u>.

The **continuous future tense** is used to refer to a future action. It is formed by using *will be* or *shall be* followed by the present participle of the main verb, often in a contracted form, as *I will be working late tonight* and *I'll be announcing the date of the exam tomorrow*.

The continuous future tense is used to describe an action that will, or is likely to, take place in the future but emphasizing that the action will go on over a period of time, or to refer events that have been planned or arranged for the future.

In the following sentences the underlined words form the **continuous future tense**:

They <u>will be changing</u> the computer system tomorrow.
He <u>will be reporting</u> the matter to the police.
The bus <u>will be changing</u> routes from tomorrow.
You <u>will be hearing</u> from my solicitors.
We <u>will be stopping</u> halfway on the journey to the city.

The **future perfect tense** is formed by using *will have* or *shall have* followed by the past participle of the main verb. It is used to predict that a future action will be completed by a particular time or to make deductions, as in:

The decorators will have finished the room by this evening.

In the following sentences the underlined words form examples of the **future perfect tense**:

They <u>will have reached</u> home by tomorrow night.
You <u>will have realized</u> by now that I am quite serious.
Shops <u>will have started</u> their sales by next week.
Doubtless she <u>will have regretted</u> her decision by tomorrow morning.

The **future perfect continuous tense** is used to refer to an action that will have been completed at a point in the future, emphasizing that the action will have been continuing over a period of time.

In the following sentences the underlined words form examples of the **future perfect continuous tense**:

Many people <u>will have been saving</u> for years for this trip.
Students <u>will have been studying</u> this text for weeks without realizing that it is the wrong one.
We <u>will have been travelling</u> for two years by the summer.

Mood

Mood is one of the categories into which verbs are divided. These **moods** are called the **indicative mood**, the **imperative mood** and the **subjunctive mood**. The word **mood** in this sense acquired its meaning because it was said to show the attitude or viewpoint that a particular verb indicated.

Indicative mood

The **indicative mood** of a verb is used to make a factual statement, as in:

They have three children.

In the following sentences the underlined words are verbs in the **indicative mood**:

The parking restrictions <u>apply</u> on working days.
It <u>snowed</u> last night.
The plane <u>leaves</u> at 7 a.m.
I <u>start</u> my new job tomorrow.
The play at the Lyceum <u>is</u> very good.
We <u>give</u> generous discounts to members of staff.
We <u>are losing</u> money on this venture.

Imperative mood

The **imperative mood** of a verb is used to give orders or instructions or to make a request, as in:

Be quiet!
Shut the door behind you.
Take care!
Bring us a copy of the menu, please.

Subjunctive mood

The **subjunctive mood** was originally a term used in Latin grammar where it was used to express a wish, supposition, doubt, improbability or other non-factual statement. The **subjunctive mood** in English is used to express hypothetical statements, as in:

If I were you I would forget all about it.

The word *were* is in the subjunctive mood. The subjunctive mood is also used in certain formal clauses beginning with *that*, as in:

I demand that she pay me in full immediately.

It is also used in certain fixed expressions, such as *So be it!*

In the following sentences the words underlined form examples of the **subjunctive mood**:

If he were to go down on bended knee I would still not forgive him.
If I were you I would leave now.

I insist that he <u>apologize</u> immediately.
<u>*Be*</u> *that as it <u>may</u>, he should still be finished.*
God <u>save</u> the Queen!
I suggest that he <u>be told</u> of our decision right away.

NB: Modern use of the subjunctive mood
The **subjunctive mood** can sound rather stilted in modern usage and many people either ignore it, perhaps being ignorant of its true use, or else choose to avoid it.

For example

I insist that he apologizes immediately

instead of

I insist that he apologize immediately

is considered quite acceptable, especially in all but the most formal contexts.

Voice

Voice with reference to verbs has nothing to do with the voice that makes sounds. Instead, it denotes two ways of looking at the action of the verb. **Transitive verbs** (*see* page 187), verbs which take an **object** (*see* page 28), can either be in the **active voice** or the **passive voice**.

Active voice

In the case of sentences using the **active voice** of the verb, the **subject** (*see* page 24) performs the action described by the verb. Thus, in the sentence

The boy threw the ball.

the verb *threw* is in the **active voice** because the **subject** of the sentence *The boy* is performing the action of throwing.

Similarly, in the sentence

She is driving the car too fast.

the verb *is driving* is in the active voice because the **subject** of the sentence *She* is performing the action of driving.

In the following sentences the underlined words form examples of verbs in the **active voice**:

Terrorists <u>hijacked</u> the plane.
Rain <u>spoiled</u> the day.
He <u>found</u> the solution.
Dad <u>dug</u> the garden.
I <u>lost</u> the ring.
A thief <u>stole</u> the purse.

Passive voice

In the case of sentences using the **passive voice** of the verb the subject is the recipient of the action of the verb. Thus, in the sentence

The ball was thrown by the boy.

the verb *was thrown* is in the **passive voice** because the **subject** of the sentence *The ball* is having the action of throwing performed on it. Similarly, in the sentence

The car was being driven too fast by her.

the verb *was being driven* is in the **passive voice** because the subject of the sentence *The car* is having the action of driving performed on it.

In the following sentences the underlined words form examples of verbs in the **passive voice**:

He <u>was</u> fatally <u>wounded</u>.
A woman <u>was found</u> dead.
The car <u>was</u> badly <u>damaged</u> in the crash.

We <u>were delighted</u> by the news.
It <u>is known</u> that a statement will be released tomorrow.

As you will see from the examples given in **Active voice** and **Passive voice** above, it is often quite easy to convert active form to passive form and vice versa.

Verbs in the **active voice** are much more commonly used in English than verbs in the passive voice. Overuse of the **passive voice** can sound rather formal and unnatural and it can make sentences sound unnecessarily complicated.

However, it should not be avoided altogether. For example, it is a useful construction when it is not yet known who carried out the action of the verb, as in:

A young man has been murdered.

It is also useful, especially to people such as journalists, in sentences such as the following where it is not known whose opinion is being given:

It is believed that such conditions may occur again.

However, this habit of generalization should not be overdone. Also, the passive construction is often used in pieces of scientific or other specialist writing where the question of who exactly is performing the action of a verb is not important, as in:

A sample of the bacterium is being tested under lab conditions.

Transitive verb and intransitive verb

We have seen above that it is only **transitive verbs** which are affected by **voice**. **Transitive verbs** are verbs which can take a **direct object** (*see* page 28). In the sentence

The men love their children.

the noun *children* is a **direct object** and the verb *love* is **transitive**. Similarly, in the sentence

The children like jelly.

the noun *jelly* is a **direct object** and the verb *like* is **transitive**. On the other hand, in the sentence

Snow fell yesterday.

the verb *fell* (*fall*) is **intransitive** because it does not take an object. Similarly, in the sentence

The situation improved.

the verb *improved* (*improve*) is **intransitive**.

Many verbs can be either **transitive** or **intransitive** according to context. Thus, in the sentence

They both play the piano.

the verb *play* is **transitive**, while, in the sentence

The children play on the beach every day.

the verb *play* is **intransitive**.

Similarly, in the sentence

They climb the highest mountains.

the verb *climb* is **transitive**, while in the sentence,

The paths climb steeply.

the verb *climb* is **intransitive**.

In the following sentences the underlined words form a **transitive verb**:

We <u>know</u> the truth.
They <u>hate</u> the climate here.
I <u>chose</u> the blue curtains.
You <u>will adore</u> him.
She <u>crossed</u> the street.
We <u>are painting</u> the house.
They <u>dig</u> the garden at weekends.
We <u>appreciate</u> the gesture.
They <u>welcome</u> the praise.
The doctor <u>cured</u> him.
We <u>want</u> more money.
They <u>drink</u> red wine.
She <u>is picking</u> flowers.

In the following sentences the underlined words form an **intransitive verb**:

A figure <u>appeared</u>.
She <u>blushes</u> easily.
These plants <u>grow</u> rapidly.
We <u>failed</u>.
They <u>work</u> hard.
He <u>died</u> yesterday.
He <u>talks</u> constantly.
Things <u>are going</u> badly.
I <u>walk</u> with difficulty.
They <u>ran</u> away.
She <u>is sleeping</u>.

Linking verb

A **linking verb**, also called a **copula** or **copular verb**, is a verb that 'links' a subject with its complement. Unlike other verbs, linking verbs do not denote an action but indicate a state.

The most common **linking verb** is *be*, as in:

He is a fool.

Others include *become, seem, appear, look*, as in:

You seemed rather an anxious person.

and

He looks a new man.

In the following sentences the underlined words form **linking verbs**:

He <u>appears</u> quite calm.
She <u>appears</u> a very competent young woman.
Mary <u>looks</u> quite exhausted.
It <u>looks</u> just what we want.
Jim <u>became</u> a famous writer.
I <u>feel</u> a different person after my holiday.
I <u>feel</u> unwell.

Auxiliary verb

An **auxiliary verb** is a verb that is used with a main verb to form certain tenses and to form a negative or question and to form the passive voice. The main **auxiliary verbs** are *be, have* and *do.* These are also known as **primary auxiliary verbs** and all three can also be used as main verbs, as in:

The house is very old.
I have a book.
and
I do a lot of work in the garden.

The verb *be* is used as an **auxiliary verb** with the *-ing* of the main verb to form the **continuous present tense** (*see* page 170), as in:

We are thinking of moving house
and
She is attending school.

The verb *be* is used with the **past participle** (*see* page 199) of the main verb to form the **passive voice** (*see* page 185), as in:

The car was parked here
and
Her hands were covered in blood.

The verb *have* is used as an **auxiliary verb** with the **past participle** (*see* page 199) of the main verb to form the **present perfect tense** and the **past perfect tense** (*see* pages 174 and 175) as in:

We have opened the box.
and
I had assumed that the two of you were old friends.

The verb *be* is used as an **auxiliary verb** with the main verb to form negative sentences, as in:

She is not accepting the job.
and
The work is not finished yet.

The verb *do* is also used as an **auxiliary verb** with the main verb to form negative sentences, as in:

I do not believe you.
and
She did not love him.

The verb *do* is also used as an **auxiliary verb** with the main verb to form questions, as in:

Do they still live here?
and
Did they go by bus?

The verb *do* is also used as an **auxiliary verb** with the main verb to emphasize the main verb, as in:

The bus does stop here, I'm sure.
and
The shop does open on Sundays.

In the following sentences the underlined words form **primary auxiliary verbs**:

He <u>does</u> still love her, he says.
<u>Does</u> the bus stop here?
She <u>doesn't</u> work here now.
The scheme <u>is</u> not operating yet.
We <u>have</u> rejected the idea.
I <u>had</u> somehow got the idea that you <u>were</u> related to him.

Modal auxiliary verb

A **modal auxiliary verb** is a verb that is used with a main verb to help it express a wide range of meanings including possibility, probability, ability, permission, prediction, obligation, suggestions, requests, invitations, offers, promises etc. The main **modal auxiliary verbs** are *can, could, may, might, will, shall, would, should, must, ought to*. **Modal auxiliary verbs**, unlike **primary auxiliary verbs**, cannot be used as main verbs, having only one form. In the following sentences the underlined words all form examples of **modal auxiliary verbs**:

The child <u>can</u> ride a bike.
She <u>could</u> stay there if she wanted to.
You <u>may</u> borrow the car if you return it by lunchtime.
We <u>may</u> be in time for the 5 o'clock train.
He <u>might</u> still have the receipt for the book.
We <u>should</u> get there before nightfall.
Those who make fraudulent claims <u>shall</u> be prosecuted.
<u>Will</u> you have some more tea?
<u>Would</u> you take a seat over there, please.
You <u>may</u> prefer to come back another time.
You <u>might</u> prefer to pay by credit card.
<u>Can</u> you post this letter for me?
<u>Could</u> you give her a message?
We <u>must</u> get there before dinner.
You <u>must</u> leave at once.
They <u>ought to</u> pay for the damage.
You <u>could</u> endanger your life by such an action.

Concord

Concord or **verb agreement** refers to the fact that a verb must 'agree' with the subject in **number**. In other words a singular subject must be accompanied by a singular verb, as in:

The boy loves chocolate.

And a plural subject must be accompanied by a plural verb, as in:

The boys love chocolate.

Concord is not a big issue in English since verbs in English generally have the same form, irrespective of **number**, apart from the change of form in the third person singular of the present tense when -*s* or -*es* is added to the base form. A difficulty arises when a subject takes the form of a singular noun linked to a plural noun by *of*, as in:

A number of problems.

Although it is grammatically correct to use a singular verb, as in the sentence

A number of problems has arisen.

it is common in modern usage to have the verb agreeing with the plural noun because it is nearest to it, this sounding more natural, as in:

A number of problems have arisen.

Sometimes it depends on whether the writer or speaker wishes to emphasize the unity of the group of things or people referred to or whether the individual components are to be emphasized. Thus, in the sentence

A collection of his paintings is to be displayed at the town hall.

the verb is singular because the paintings are being regarded as a single entity. However, in the sentence

A collection of miscellaneous valuable objects were found in the thief's house.

the verb is in the plural form because the emphasis is on the number of individual objects. This duality of singular and plural verbs also arises with regard to some **collective nouns** (*see* page 93).Thus in the sentence

The family is what matters most to her.

the verb is singular, whereas in the sentence

The family are coming from all parts of the world to be home for Christmas.

the verb is plural.

Parts of a verb

Infinitive

The **infinitive**, or **base**, is the form of a verb when used without any indication of person, number or tense. There are two forms of the infinitive. One is the **to infinitive** form, as in:

They wished <u>to leave</u>.
The child has nothing <u>to do</u>.

The other form of the **infinitive**, without *to*, is sometimes called the **base infinitive**. This form consists of the base form of the verb without *to*, as in:

We saw him <u>fall</u>. and *She watched him <u>go</u>.*

> **NB: The split infinitive**
> The **split infinitive** is an infinitive that has had another word in the form of an **adverb** placed between itself and *to*, as in
>
> *to rudely push*
> and
> *to quietly accept*.
>
> This was once considered a bad grammatical error, but the split infinitive is becoming acceptable in modern usage. In any case, it sometimes makes for a clumsy sentence if one slavishly follows the correct form.

Participles

There are two **participles**. One is the **present participle** which is formed by adding the ending *-ing* to the **base** or **infinitive form**, as in *going*. If the base form ends in *-e*, the *-e* is usually removed before the -ing ending is added, as *making*. The other is the **past participle** which is formed by adding the ending *-ed* to the **base** or **infinitive** form.

Present participle

The **present participle** is used with parts of the verb *be* to form the **continuous present tense** (*see* page 170) and other continuous tenses, as in:

I am waiting.
and
She was watching.

The **present participle** can also function as an **adjective**, positioned next to the noun which it modifies.
   In the following phrases the underlined word is a **present participle** functioning as an **adjective**:

no <u>running</u> water
the <u>sinking</u> ship
the <u>protesting</u> crowd
the <u>whispering</u> onlookers
the <u>crumbling</u> sea wall
a <u>disappearing</u> way of life

a <u>fading</u> memory
the <u>driving</u> rain.

The **present participle** can also function as a noun. (*see* **verbal noun**, page 90).

The **present participle** is also used in **participial phrases** (*see* page 71).

Past participle

In **regular verbs**, the **past participle** has the same form as the **past tense** (*see* page 171). In the case of **irregular verbs,** however, the **past participle** is formed in different ways.

The **past participle** is used with parts of the verb *have* to form the **perfect tense** (*see* page 174) and other perfect tenses.

The **past participle** is also used in **participial phrases** (*see* page 72).

EXERCISES 5

1 Which of the following are parts of **regular verbs**?

walked, looked, stuck, met, smiled, kept, held, seemed, hated, meant, climbed, drew, loved, begun, laughed, worked, felt, called, fought, rained, snowed.

2 Write down the **past tense** of the following **irregular verbs**.

do, swim, drink, fly, rise, blow, tear, throw, write, shut, choose, tell, think, understand, dig, find, send, build, cut, hit, make, grow, ring, speak, break, wear, give, know, steal.

3 The following sentences contain underlined verbs in the **past tense**. Rewrite the sentences to contain the same verbs but in the **continuous past tense**.

The man <u>stood</u> outside the shop.
The church bells <u>rang</u> out.
The children <u>slept</u> peacefully.
The mother <u>rocked</u> the cradle slowly.
The sun <u>shone</u> brightly from very early in the morning.
They <u>walked</u> as fast as they could.
I <u>studied</u> English at university.

4 Which of the following underlined verbs are in the **future tense**?

We <u>will go</u> immediately.
I <u>am cleaning</u> the house just now.
They <u>will need</u> a visa to cross the border.
The project <u>will cost</u> a lot of money.
He <u>was sure</u> of success.
She <u>is about to leave</u> on a dangerous journey.
We <u>have finished</u> the job.
Things <u>are going to improve</u> soon.
I <u>will consult</u> my solicitor shortly.
They <u>are going to submit</u> an application.
The luggage was damaged during the flight.

5 Which of the following underlined verbs are in the **subjunctive mood,** which are in the **imperative mood** and which are in the **indicative mood**?

If I <u>were</u> the head teacher, I would exclude the bullies immediately.
<u>Get out</u> now!
He <u>sells</u> a wide range of electrical goods.
The parking regulations <u>apply</u> only in the city centre.
<u>Watch out</u>!
We <u>walk</u> to work every morning.
I suggest that the students' lockers <u>be searched</u> for the stolen goods.
It <u>rained</u> all last week.
I demand that you <u>give</u> me <u>back</u> the money immediately.
<u>Stop</u> thief!
I <u>believe</u> him.

6 In the following sentences which of the underlined verbs are in the **active voice** and which are in the **passive voice**?

Rain is spoiling the picnic.
He was driving the lorry dangerously.
She was supported by her husband.
Someone has stolen a valuable painting from the art gallery.
A bicycle has been stolen from the shop by a gang of youths.
The severe storm destroyed the crops.
The whole village was devastated by the tragedy.
We are digging a new flower garden.
The ancient artefact was found by a farmer in his field.
The floods damaged a great deal of property.
The ball was thrown over the hedge by the boy.
A new office system is being tested right now.

7 In the following sentences which verbs are **transitive** and which are **intransitive**?

Snow fell that night.
They need a place to live.
They painted the front door.
Things went well.
A man suddenly appeared.
They welcomed their guests warmly.

We were picking wild flowers.
Their guests drank only water.
The tree grew rapidly.
Doctors could not cure the patient.
We worked all night.
The child chose two library books.
She died about a year ago.
Few people know the real facts.
He can't walk without a stick now.

8 Write out the sentences which contain a **linking verb**, underlining each of the linking verbs.

The ghost, apparently, appeared last night.
She appears a different person since her counselling sessions.
We looked carefully at samples.
He looked in the mirror.
She looks a suitable enough candidate for the job.
She says that she feels a completely new person since her short break.
Jack became a lawyer.
They seem fine young people.
His brother is a doctor.
She is an attractive young woman.
Her father appeared to her in a dream.
It seems an appropriate solution.
We looked over a few houses.

9 Write out the sentences which contain a **modal auxiliary verb**, underlining each of the modal auxiliary verbs.

Could you give me some assistance?
She does have talent.
They might get there in time, if the traffic's light.
Jack did know the accident victim.
She should pass the driving test first time.
She has lost her memory.
Dad says that we may borrow the car.
She is taking great care of them.
They could lose a lot of money in this venture.
I can't meet you today.
The task is not finished yet.
Would you come this way, please?
Can you sign here, please?
We are studying the evidence.
Might we discuss this at a more convenient time?

10 Write out the sentences which contain the **base infinitive** of a verb, underlining each base infinitive.

I heard him go.
We wished him to leave.
We watched the children play.
I have to go now.
He saw her die.

Have you something important to say?
I want you to give me some advice.
Did you see him attack her?
They aimed to leave right away.
We both heard someone drive past the house.
Many older workers plan to take early retirement.
Two people witnessed the man fall from the bridge.

ANSWERS 5

1 *walked, looked, smiled, seemed, hated, climbed, loved, laughed, worked, called, rained, snowed.*

2 *did, swam, drank, flew, rose, blew, tore, threw, wrote, shut, chose, told, thought, understood, dug, found, sent, built, cut, hit, made, grew, rang, spoke, broke, wore, gave, knew, stole.*

3 *The man <u>was standing</u> outside the shop.*
The church bells <u>were ringing</u> out.
The children <u>were sleeping</u> peacefully.
The mother <u>was rocking</u> the cradle slowly.
The sun <u>was shining</u> brightly from very early in the morning.
They <u>were walking</u> as fast as they could.
I <u>was studying</u> English at university.

4 **future tense** *will go, will need, will cost, is about to leave, are going to improve, will consult, are going to submit.*

5 **subjunctive mood** *were, be searched, give back.*
imperative mood *get out, watch out, stop.*
indicative mood *sells, apply, walk, rained, believe.*

6 active voice *is spoiling, was driving, has stolen, destroyed, are digging, damaged.*
passive voice *was murdered, has been stolen, was devastated, was found, was thrown, is being tested.*

7 transitive *need, painted, welcomed, picking, drank, cure, chose, know.*
intransitive *fell, went, appeared, grew, worked, died, walk.*

8 *She <u>appears</u> a different person since her counselling sessions.*
She <u>looks</u> a suitable enough candidate for the job.
She says that she <u>feels</u> a completely new person since her short break.
Jack <u>became</u> a lawyer.
They <u>seem</u> fine young people.
His brother <u>is</u> a doctor.
She <u>is</u> an attractive young woman.
It <u>seems</u> an appropriate solution.

9 *<u>Could</u> you give me some assistance?*
They <u>might</u> get there in time, if the traffic's light.
She <u>should</u> pass the driving test first time.
Dad says that we <u>may</u> borrow the car.
They <u>could</u> lose a lot of money in this venture.
I <u>can't</u> meet you today.

Would you come this way, please?
Can you sign here, please?
Might we discuss this at a more convenient time?

10 I heard him *go*.
We watched the children *play*.
He saw her *die*.
Did you see him *attack* her?
We both heard someone *drive* past the house.
Two people witnessed the man *fall* from the bridge.

PARTS OF SPEECH IV

Adverbs

The main function of an **adverb** is to give more information about a verb. An **adverb** is said to **modify** a verb
because it limits the word it describes in some way. Thus,
modifying the verb *walk* with the adverb *quickly* means
that we know that we are concentrating on walking
quickly and that we can forget about walking in any other
way. **Adverbs** can also modify other adverbs, as in
extremely suddenly, adjectives, as in *gravely ill*, prepositions, as in *just after dinner* and conjunctions as in *exactly
what he said*.

An **adverb** is usually a single word. When a group
of words performs the same function as an adverb
it is known as an **adverbial phrase** or **adverbial** (*see*
page 69).

Types of adverb

There are various types of **adverb**—adverbs of **time**,
frequency, **duration**, **place**, **manner** and **degree,** as
well as **interrogative** adverbs.

Adverbs of time

Adverbs of time indicate when something has
happened. They include words such as *then, now,
afterwards, before, later*. In the following sentences the
underlined words are **adverbs of time**:

I'll see you <u>soon.</u>
They haven't seen him <u>lately</u>.
It was her birthday <u>today</u>.
I wasn't married <u>then</u>.
We'd never met <u>before</u>.
<u>Afterwards</u> we had afternoon tea.

Adverbs of frequency

Adverbs of frequency indicate how frequently something happens. They include words such as *often*, *always* , *never*, and *seldom*.

In the following sentences the underlined words are **adverbs of frequency**:

It <u>always</u> snowed at Christmas there.
We <u>rarely</u> meet these days.
He <u>never</u> drinks alcohol.
She is <u>forever</u> criticizing him.
We play tennis together <u>regularly</u>.
The patient is being monitored <u>constantly</u>.
We <u>usually</u> have dinner at 8 p.m.

Adverbs of duration

Adverbs of duration indicate how long something lasts or occurs. They include words such as *always, briefly, permanently, indefinitely*.

In the following sentences the underlined words are **adverbs of duration**:

She is living with her grandmother <u>temporarily</u>.
He has been suspended from his job <u>indefinitely</u>.
I haven't known her <u>long</u>.
We will stay here <u>overnight</u>.
She's <u>always</u> lived here.
They stopped <u>briefly</u> to fill the car with petrol.

Adverbs of place

Adverbs of place are used to indicate where something happens or takes place. They include such words as *here, there, near, downstairs* and *indoors*.

In the following sentences the underlined words are **adverbs of place**:

He has gone <u>overseas</u>.
They live <u>nearby</u>.
She went <u>inside</u>.
He walked <u>alongside</u>.
They are travelling <u>northward</u>.
We waded <u>ashore</u>.
The child doesn't live <u>here</u>.
He held the banner <u>aloft</u>.
We met <u>midway</u>.

Adverbs of manner

Adverbs of manner indicate how something happens or the circumstances in which something happens. They are frequently formed by adding -*ly* to an adjective and they include *carefully, easily, hurriedly, plainly, quickly, safely, suddenly, willingly*. A few of them end in *-wise, -ways* or *-wards*.

In the following sentences the underlined words are **adverbs of manner**:

She was <u>neatly</u> dressed.
He smiled <u>vaguely</u>.
They spoke <u>eloquently</u>.
I behaved <u>foolishly</u>.
He lives <u>dangerously</u>.
We waited <u>patiently</u>.
You are needed <u>urgently</u>.
She laughed <u>excitedly</u>.
They filmed him <u>secretly</u>.
I met him <u>accidentally</u>.
She acted <u>independently</u>.
He moved <u>sideways</u>.

Adverbs of degree

Adverbs of degree are used to indicate the degree to which an action is performed. Many of them are formed by adding *-ly* to an adjective and they include *fairly, moderately, remarkably, very* and *partly*.

In the following sentences the underlined words are **adverbs of degree**:

I enjoyed the film <u>immensely</u>.
I was <u>tremendously</u> pleased by the unexpected gift.
She was <u>hugely</u> impressed by the efforts of the children.

She was <u>unbelievably</u> beautiful.
They were only <u>moderately</u> enthusiastic about the project.
She was <u>slightly</u> hurt by the remark.
They were <u>partly</u> responsible for the error.
Her father was a <u>supremely</u> successful businessman.
They <u>largely</u> ignored us.
The village was <u>virtually</u> destroyed by the storms.
The child <u>almost</u> drowned.
I was <u>enormously</u> encouraged by their praise.
He was working <u>very</u> hard.

Adverbs of emphasis

A small group of **adverbs of degree** are known as **adverbs of emphasis**. These are formed from **emphatic adjectives** and include *absolutely*, *entirely, really, utterly* and *positively.*

In the following sentences the underlined words are **adverbs of emphasis**:

We <u>totally</u> disagree with you.
I was <u>utterly</u> devastated by the news.
I <u>quite</u> agree.
She <u>positively</u> adores him.
He <u>really</u> loathes his job.
She <u>completely</u> broke down and wept uncontrollably.

Interrogative adverbs

Interrogative adverbs are among the **wh- words** which

are used to ask **wh- questions** (*see* page 37) and include *when, where, how* and *why*.

In the following sentences the underlined words are **interrogative adverbs**:

<u>*When*</u> *did you last see him?*
<u>*Where*</u> *was the money hidden?*
<u>*How*</u> *are you feeling?*
<u>*Why*</u> *was he there?*

Prepositions

A **preposition** is used to show the relationship, such as time or place, between a noun or pronoun and the rest of a sentence, clause or phrase. The **preposition** usually comes before the noun it refers to or 'governs'. There are two types of preposition, **simple prepositions** and **complex prepositions**.

Simple prepositions

Simple prepositions are often very short words, such as *at, by, in, of, off, on, to* and *up*, but also include such words as *among, before, behind, during* and *through*.

In the following sentences the underlined words are all **simple prepositions**:

The cakes are <u>on</u> the table.
The cat is <u>up</u> the tree.
She sleeps <u>during</u> the day.
They left <u>before</u> dawn.
We arrived <u>after</u> dinner.
I will stay there <u>for</u> three weeks.
He is a young man <u>of</u> great talent.
She carried a bag <u>with</u> a black handle.
I will go <u>with</u> them.
He was sacked <u>for</u> theft.
I paid <u>by</u> cash.
We had to leave <u>without</u> Mary.
They were <u>against</u> the scheme.

Complex prepositions

Complex prepositions consist of two or three words. These include *ahead of, because of, instead of, on account of, by means of* and *on behalf of*.

In the following sentences the underlined words form **complex prepositions**:

She attended the conference <u>in spite of</u> illness.
He had to retire <u>on account of</u> his age.
They are not rich <u>in terms of</u> money.
They have a dog <u>in addition to</u> the three cats.

Conjunctions

A **conjunction** is a linking word used to join words, word groups or **clauses** (*see* page 53). There are two types of conjunction, **coordinating conjunctions** and **subordinating conjunctions**.

Coordinating conjunctions

Coordinating conjunctions are conjunctions which join elements which are of equal status. These units may be words, word groups or main clauses. **Coordinating conjunctions** include *and, but, or, yet* and, in pairs and often for emphasis, *both … and, either … or, neither … nor.*

In the following sentences the underlined words **are coordinating conjunctions** which link words:

The women <u>and</u> children left the sinking ship first.
She's an artist <u>and</u> a writer.
He was wearing a hat <u>and</u> gloves.
He is an intelligent <u>and</u> enthusiastic young man.
It was a difficult <u>and</u> embarrassing problem.
The firm was being run efficiently <u>and</u> economically.
He was tall, dark <u>and</u> handsome.
She was poor <u>but</u> happy.
It was a small <u>but</u> comfortable house.
She was elderly <u>but</u> extremely fit.
They worked slowly <u>but</u> confidently.
You can serve fruit <u>or</u> cheese at the end of the meal.
Did you <u>or</u> your husband witness the crime?
Is that good <u>or</u> bad news?

The teacher was firm yet fair.
She was both pretty and clever.
He is both a coward and a bully.
They are either stupid or naïve.
She is either foolish or deceitful.
They are neither skilled nor experienced.
We have neither sufficient money nor sufficient time to undertake this task.

In the following sentences the underlined words are **coordinating conjunctions** which link main clauses:

He has asked Anne to marry him and she has accepted.
The students live in Leeds and they travel here every day.
He was born in England but lives in Australia.
They can stay here or they can go home.
Students can either live in flats or they can live in halls of residence.

Subordinating conjunctions

Subordinating conjunctions are used to link a **subordinate clause** or dependent clause (*see* page 54) to the **main clause**. **Subordinating conjunctions** may introduce an **adverbial clause**, a **comparative clause**, a **relative clause**, or a **noun clause**. For all of these *see* pages 53–67.

Subordinating conjunctions introducing adverbial clauses

These are **clauses** which have a function in a sentence similar to that of an **adverb** (*see* pages 209–214) or an

adverbial phrase (*see* page 69). They add information about time, place, concession, condition, manner, purpose and result.

Subordinating conjunctions introducing adverbial clauses of time include *after, before, since, when, whenever, while, until, as soon as*. In the following sentences the underlined word/words form a conjunction introducing an adverbial clause of time:

<u>As soon as</u> the babysitter comes we'll set off.
I smile <u>whenever</u> I see the child's happy face.
I'll wait <u>until</u> your friend comes.

Subordinating conjunctions introducing adverbial clauses of place include *where, wherever, everywhere*. In the following sentences the underlined word is a conjunction introducing an adverbial clause of place:

I forget <u>where</u> I left the package.
<u>Wherever</u> the actor goes, photographers follow.

Subordinating conjunctions introducing adverbial clauses of purpose include *in order (to), to, so as to, so that*. In the following sentences the underlined word/words form a conjunction introducing an adverbial clause of purpose:

We left the party early <u>so as to</u> catch the last bus home.
<u>To</u> get there on time we'd have to leave now.
I saved money all year <u>so that</u> I could afford to go on holiday to South Africa.

Subordinating conjunctions introducing adverbial clauses of reason include *because, since, as, in case*. In the following sentences the underlined word/words form a conjunction introducing an adverbial clause of reason:

We need to leave very early <u>in case</u> the traffic is very heavy on the motorway.
<u>Because</u> it's raining heavily we'll have to cancel the picnic.
<u>Since</u> he committed the crime he should accept the punishment.

Subordinating conjunctions introducing adverbial clauses of result include *so that*. The words *so* and *that* can be separated, *so* coming before an adjective or adverb in the main clause and *that* being the first word in the subordinate clause. In the following sentences the underlined word/words form a conjunction introducing an adverbial clause of result:

He hit his opponent <u>so</u> hard <u>that</u> he knocked him out.
He spoke clearly <u>so that</u> everyone heard every word.

Subordinating conjunctions introducing adverbial clauses of condition include *unless, if, provided (that), providing, as long as*. In the following sentences the underlined word/words form a conjunction introducing an adverbial clause of condition:

I'll go <u>provided</u> you come with me.
<u>As long as</u> you're happy I'm happy to do what you ask.
<u>If</u> he stays I'm leaving.

Subordinating conjunctions introducing adverbial clauses of manner include *as though, as if, as, like*. In the following sentences the underlined word/words form a conjunction introducing an adverbial clause of manner:

He walked <u>as though</u> he were in pain.
She smiled broadly <u>as if</u> she were very happy.

Subordinating conjunctions introducing adverbial clauses of concession include *although, though, even though, whereas, while, whilst*. In the following sentences the underlined word/words form a conjunction introducing an adverbial clause of concession:

She still loves him <u>although</u> he treated her badly.
<u>Even though</u> I dislike him personally I admire his work.
<u>While</u> Mary is an excellent cook neither of her sisters can even boil an egg.

EXERCISES 6

1 Write out the sentences which contain an adverb, underlining the adverbs.

She was very pretty.
He was smartly dressed.
The man is an utter fool.
He utterly adores her.
She enjoyed her time at university tremendously.
The campaign was a huge success.
He was once a supremely successful chef.
It was a regular occurrence.
He acted impulsively and foolishly.
She was not in a very patient mood.
We go to the cinema regularly.
They rarely meet.
I usually go to work by train.
We go to France in the summer.
They went to their usual restaurant in the high street.
She stamped her foot impatiently.

2 Write down the adverbs of duration and the adverbs of frequency in the following sentences.

Jack never tells lies.
I worry about him constantly.
The couple plan to leave here permanently.
Sue is forever talking of looking for another job.

They stopped over briefly in Singapore on their way to Australia.
We seldom see our old friends.
The boys often play football on Saturdays.
She is working as a secretary temporarily.
Are you going to work in the States indefinitely?

3 Rewrite the following sentences inserting in the blanks an adverb formed from the adjective given in bold type in brackets.

*I met her ... on the way to the station. (**accidental**)*
*He won ... and went on to the next round. (**easy**)*
*You must proceed ... and be aware of the danger. (**careful**)*
*She acted ... without thinking. (**foolish**)*
*He left his job quite ... in a panic. (**sudden**)*
*You have to decide ... if you want the job. (**quick**)*

4 Write out the following sentences, underlining the simple prepositions.

I stayed there for six months.
She is a person of considerable wealth.
She did the shopping during her lunch hour.
They live in the house with the green door.
I will pay by cheque.
The money is on the kitchen table.
The workman is up the ladder.
She studies during the evening.

I'm leaving after breakfast.
If we leave now we'll get there before the bus.
She directed the remark at him.
She thought he was the man of her dreams.

5 Write out the sentences which contain a complex preposition, underlining the complex prepositions.

He was invited, but his sister went instead.
My colleague was ill and so I went to the conference instead of her.
He had to take early retirement on account of his ill health.
He won the race in spite of his injured back.
I can't pay for the work in full, but here is some money on account.
He has promised to speak for her at the complaints tribunal.
The union leader is going to talk to management on behalf of all the workers.
You can get there by means of transport, but it will take a long time.
Let's go by train.
She resigned because of acute stress.
She must have gone for her own reasons.

6 Write out the sentences which contain a coordinating conjunction, underlining each of the coordinating conjunctions.

The girls and boys go into the school by different entrances.
You can have either tea or coffee.
I'll wait till they turn up.
We decided not to go because of the rain.
She was very old but in good health.
I know when to leave.
Did you or your brother see your mother before you left for school?
I get angry whenever I catch sight of him.
He is hard-working and experienced.
She is either his cousin or his aunt, I'm not sure which.
He forgot what he said.
If he does that he'll be sacked.
Usually they go to France for the summer but they are going to Italy this year.
He asked her to marry him and she accepted.
He cycled to work in order to get fit.
They can rent an apartment or they can stay in a budget hotel.

7 Underline the subordinating conjunctions in the following sentences.

We realized that he was quite ill.
She sang while he played the piano.
Although he is very talented he has been unable to find a job.
If you leave now you will get the last bus.
I'll tell them the good news as soon as I see them.

I'll get there before dinner provided the traffic is not too heavy.

After dinner he was so tired that he fell asleep in his chair.

While she is highly academically qualified, she has very little experience.

Since it's raining very heavily the beach picnic will have to be cancelled.

She's been going to that seaside resort since she was a child.

We'll set out as soon as it stops raining.

Why did she go I wonder?

The students won't pass the exams unless they study hard.

ANSWERS 6

1 *She was <u>very</u> pretty.*
He was <u>smartly</u> dressed.
He <u>utterly</u> adores her.
She enjoyed her time at university <u>tremendously</u>.
He was once a <u>supremely</u> successful chef.
He acted <u>impulsively</u> and <u>foolishly</u>.
She was not in a <u>very</u> patient mood.
We go to the cinema <u>regularly</u>.
They <u>rarely</u> meet.
I <u>usually</u> go to work by train.
She stamped her foot <u>impatiently</u>.

2 **adverbs of duration** *permanently, briefly, temporarily, indefinitely*
adverbs of frequency *never, constantly, forever, seldom, often*

3 *I met her **accidentally** on the way to the station.*
*He won **easily** and went on to the next round.*
*You must proceed **carefully** and be aware of the danger.*
*She acted **foolishly** without thinking.*
*He left his job quite **suddenly** in a panic.*
*You have to decide **quickly** if you want the job.*

4 *I stayed there <u>for</u> six months.*
She is a person <u>of</u> considerable wealth.
She did the shopping <u>during</u> her lunch hour.
They live in the house <u>with</u> the green door.
I will pay <u>by</u> cheque.
The money is <u>on</u> the kitchen table.
The workman is <u>up</u> the ladder.
She studies <u>during</u> the evening.
I'm leaving <u>after</u> breakfast.
If we leave now we'll get there <u>before</u> the bus.
She directed the remark <u>at</u> him.
She thought he was the man <u>of</u> her dreams.

5 *My colleague was ill and so I went to the conference <u>instead of</u> her.*
He had to take early retirement <u>on account of</u> his ill health.
He won the race <u>in spite of</u> his injured back.
The union leader is going to talk to management <u>on behalf of</u> all the workers.
You can get there <u>by means of</u> public transport, but it will take a long time.
She resigned <u>because of</u> acute stress.

6 *The girls <u>and</u> boys go into the school by different entrances.*

You can have either tea <u>or</u> coffee.

She was very old <u>but</u> in good health.

Did you <u>or</u> your brother see your mother before you left for school?

He is hard-working <u>and</u> experienced.

She is <u>either</u> his cousin <u>or</u> his aunt, I'm not sure which.

Usually they go to France for the summer <u>but</u> they are going to Italy this year.

He asked her to marry him <u>and</u> she accepted.

They can rent an apartment <u>or</u> they can stay in a budget hotel.

7 *We realized <u>that</u> he was quite ill.*

She sang <u>while</u> he played the piano.

<u>Although</u> he is very talented he has been unable to find a job.

<u>If</u> you leave now you will get the last bus.

I'll tell them the good news <u>as soon as</u> I see them.

I'll get there before dinner <u>provided</u> the traffic is not too heavy.

After dinner he was <u>so</u> tired <u>that</u> he fell asleep in his chair.

<u>While</u> she is highly academically qualified, she has very little experience.

<u>Since</u> it's raining very heavily, the beach picnic will have to be cancelled.

She's been going to that seaside resort <u>since</u> she was a child.

We'll set out <u>as soon as</u> it stops raining.

<u>Why </u>did she go I wonder?

The students won't pass the exams <u>unless</u> they study hard.

Punctuation

THE IMPORTANCE OF PUNCTUATION

Punctuation is the use of certain established marks (**punctuation marks**) or symbols within a piece of written text. **Punctuation** prevents a piece of text from being just a string of words by breaking up the string of words into meaningful units and by making the text more fluent. Basically, punctuation marks can be seen as symbols which are used to separate and join units of language into a cohesive text.

Modern writers tend to punctuate much more lightly than their older counterparts did. This goes hand in hand with the modern tendency to use less formal language and a plainer style. However, the importance of punctuation, even in these less formal modern times, should not be underestimated. Appropriate punctuation creates order in what might otherwise be a piece of linguistic confusion.

The important punctuation marks are the **full stop**, **question mark**, **exclamation mark**, **comma**, **brackets**, **dash**, **semicolon**, **colon**, **hyphen**, **quotation marks**, **apostrophe**, **asterisk**, **three-dot ellipsis** and the **oblique**.

Full stop

The **full stop**, also called **period**, is a punctuation mark consisting of a small dot (.). It is one of the most important punctuation marks and the most emphatic, because its main function is to mark the end of a sentence and so separate one sentence from another. Only sentences that are either **questions** or **exclamations** (*see* pages 36 and 40) do not end in a **full stop**. Instead, they end respectively in a **question mark** or an **exclamation mark**. The following are examples of sentences ending in a full stop:

The children behaved very well.
They are getting married next week.
We are moving house soon.
The car broke down.
You can choose the restaurant.
I went by bus.

NB: The stop
The **full stop** is also used to mark the end of a group of words which is not actually a sentence, but which is complete in itself, as in the following underlined words.

'When do we leave?'
'Tomorrow morning.'

The full stop and abbreviations

The **full stop** has another function. It is used with certain types of **abbreviation**, although the modern tendency, particularly in British English, is to use full stops with abbreviations far less than was formerly the case. For example, abbreviations involving initial capital letters are generally written without full stops, especially in British English, as *TUC, BBC, USA*. In such cases full stops should definitely not be used if one or some of the initial letters do not belong to a full word, as *TV. TV* is the abbreviation for television and the letter *V* is simply the initial letter of the second syllable of the word, not that of a new word.

There are usually no **full stops** in abbreviations involving the first and last letters of a word (**contractions**), as *Dr, Rd, St*, but whether they are used or not can be a matter of taste. The important thing is to be consistent in whether you use **full stops** or not in such cases.Abbreviations involving the first few letters of a word are the most likely to have **full stops**, as in *Feb*. for February and *Sept*. for September.

The full stop in email and website addresses

The **full stop** is also used in **email addresses** such as

sample.name@sampleaddress.co.uk

and in **website addresses** such as

www.sample-url.com

In these cases the inclusion of the full stops and their correct placing are necessary to send the email successfully or access the website.

Question mark

The **question mark (?)** is sometimes also known as the **query** and it is used to mark the end of a sentence which asks a question (*see* page 36). The following sentences are all questions ending in a **question mark**:

Where are we?
Is that the right time?
Who is that?
Why did they leave so early?
Does he always behave so badly?
Would you pass me the salt, please?
Can I help you?
Whose coat is this?

NB: Writing questions
It is not recommended to use more than one question mark at the end of a sentence.
   When writing college essays or literary interpretations it may be tempting to interperse your writing with questions, as in:

'So what do we learn from Wordsworth's view of nature?'

This is too informal for a such a composition. It is better to write:

'What we learn from Wordsworth's view of nature is ...'

Exclamation mark

The **exclamation mark** (!) is used to mark the end of
an **exclamation** or sometimes a **directive** (*see* page 39).
The following sentences are all exclamations or directives ending in an **exclamation mark**:

Run!
Save me!
What a beautiful day!
How marvellous!
Well done!
You must be joking!
Ouch!
Let me go!

NB: Watch out!
Be careful not to overuse the **exclamation mark**.
It is easy to do so, particularly in a piece of
informal English. One is enough at the close of a
sentence. Overuse of such sentences within a
piece of writing can detract from the potential
dramatic effect of the occasional use of the mark.

It is common for people to overuse exclamation
marks in emails, because the communication is
often informal and because we are often trying to
convey points of view and emotions that we
would not normally be doing in a formal piece of
writing.

Capital letter

Capital letters are not technically speaking punctuation marks, but their use is so closely associated with the use of the **full stop**, and with the **question mark** and **exclamation mark** that it makes sense to treat their use here. Just as a sentence ends with a **full stop** or, occasionally, with a **question mark** or **exclamation mark**, so it always begins with a **capital letter**. The opposite of a **capital letter** is a **lower-case letter** (*see* next page). **Capital letters** are used in a number of situations:

A **capital letter is** used as the initial letter **of the first word** of a sentence or a direct quotation, as in *They left early.* and *He said weakly, 'I don't feel very well.'*

A **capital letter** is always used as the initial letter of a name or proper noun, as in *Mary Brown*, *South America*, *Rome*, *speak Italian*, *Buddhism and Marxism*.

A **capital letter** is also used as the initial letter of the main words in the titles of people, places or works of art, as in the following:

Uncle Fred, *Professor Jones*, *Ely Cathedral*, *Edinburgh University*, *Glasgow Caledonian University*, *reading* Wuthering Heights, *watching a production of* Guys and Dolls, *listen to Beethoven's Third Symphony* and *buy a copy of 'The Potato Eaters' by van Gogh*.

They are also used in the titles of wars and historical, cultural and geological periods, as in the *Wars of the Roses, the Renaissance* and *the Ice Age*. Only the major words of titles, etc, begin with capital letters. Words, such as *the, on, of,* etc, are in lower-case letters, as *The Mill on the Floss*.

A **capital letter** is used as the initial letter of the days of the week, months of the year, and religious festivals, as *Monday, October, Easter, Yom Kippur*. It is a matter of choice whether the seasons of the year are given capital letters or not, as in spring/Spring, autumn/ Autumn.

A **capital letter** is used as the initial letter of God, Allah or Jesus Christ, or similar words. When a pronoun is used to refer to God or Christ the pronoun begins with an initial capital letter, as *God asks us to trust in Him*.

A **capital letter** is always used as the initial letter of a noun that is a trade name as in *Peugeot, Xerox, Hoover*. When verbs are formed from such nouns, they are usually spelt with an initial **lower-case letter** (*see* below), as in *xerox the letter* and *hoover the carpet*.

Lower-case letter

The opposite of a **capital letter** is a **lower-case letter**, also known informally as **small letter**. **Lower-case letters** are used for most words in the language. It is **capital letters** that are exceptional in their use.

EXERCISES 7

1 Rewrite the following passages, inserting the appropriate **punctuation mark** at the end of each sentence.

a

Ouch I slipped on the ice and hurt my ankle I can hardly walk Do you think my ankle could be broken
Perhaps I'd better get a doctor to have a look at it Could you possibly take me to the hospital in your car if you've time It shouldn't take very long, should it It's not far If you're in a hurry you can just drop me outside the hospital and leave I'll phone my parents from the hospital and they'll come and get me

b

Is that the right time It's much later than I thought and we simply mustn't miss the nine o'clock train It's the last one tonight Isn't that it standing at the platform Come on Run We may just catch it if we're lucky We made it just in time Thank goodness We'd better phone home to say we're on our way or Mum will be worried You know what she's like

c

I don't know many people at this party That man over there looks familiar, though Do you know who he is I seem to recognize the woman he's with as well Who can she be Where's our host I'll just go and ask him who they are I don't see them anymore Have they gone How annoying Never mind I probably didn't know them anyway They probably just looked like some other people I know

2 Rewrite the following passages replacing a **lower-case letter** with a **capital letter** where you think this is appropriate.

a
it's saturday today and we're going shopping. christmas is only two weeks away and we've still got a lot of gifts to buy, although we bought quite a few in november. we want to find something special for my sister anne. she's been working in south africa and we haven't seen her since easter last year. anne's arriving at heathrow next tuesday and my brother john and I are going to the airport to meet her. we live in london and so we don't have far to go, although we'll probably get caught up in traffic jams.

b
They all teach english at american universities and they've come to britain to attend a conference in oxford. after the conference ends they're planning to go on a brief tour of britain. They'll start with stratford and they have tickets for performances of shakespeare's king lear *and* twelfth

night. *Then they're going to london and plan to go on a river cruise on the thames before going to the tower of london and windsor castle. after that they're going to go to canterbury and then to ely to visit the cathedrals there before travelling up to scotland to attend some of the events at the edinburgh festival in august. they hope to have time to go to the various art exhibitions, particularly the one featuring the impressionists.*

1

a

Ouch! I slipped on the ice and hurt my ankle. I can hardly walk. Do you think my ankle could be broken? Perhaps I'd better get a doctor to have a look at it. Could you possibly take me to the hospital in your car if you've time? It shouldn't take very long, should it? It's not far. If you're in a hurry you can just drop me outside the hospital and leave. I'll phone my parents from the hospital and they'll come and get me.

b

Is that the right time? It's much later than I thought and we simply mustn't miss the nine o'clock train.
It's the last one tonight. Isn't that it standing at the platform? Come on! Run! We may just catch it if we're lucky. We made it just in time. Thank goodness! We'd better phone home to say we're on our way or Mum will be worried. You know what she's like.

c

I don't know many people at this party. That man over there looks familiar, though. Do you know who he is? I seem to recognize the woman he's with as well. Who can she be? Where's our host? I'll just go and ask him who they are. I don't see them anymore. Have they gone? How annoying! Never mind! I probably didn't know them anyway. They probably just looked like some other people I know.

2

a

It's Saturday today and we're going shopping. Christmas is only two weeks away and we've still got a lot of gifts to buy, although we bought quite a few in November. We want to find something special for my sister Anne. She's been working in South Africa and we haven't seen her since Easter last year. Anne's arriving at Heathrow next Tuesday and my brother John and I are going to the airport to meet her. We live in London and so we don't have far to go, although we'll probably get caught up in traffic jams.

b

They all teach English at American universities and they've come to Britain to attend a conference in Oxford. After the conference ends they're planning to go on a brief tour of Britain. They'll start with Stratford and they have tickets for performances of Shakespeare's King Lear *and* Twelfth Night. *Then they're going to London and plan to go on a river cruise on the Thames before going to the Tower of London and Windsor Castle. After that they're going to go to Canterbury and then to Ely to visit the cathedrals there before travelling up to Scotland to attend some of the events at the Edinburgh Festival in August. They hope to have time to go to the various art exhibitions, particularly the one featuring the Impressionists.*

Comma

A **comma** (,) is an extremely common punctuation mark and yet the use of **commas** causes a great deal of concern and confusion in many people. This is partly because the use of commas has changed quite a bit in recent times.

In modern usage there is a tendency to adopt a system of minimal punctuation and one of the casualties of this change has been the comma. Most people use the comma considerably less frequently than was formerly the case.

The **comma** has two major functions, that of linking and separating.

The comma as separating device in lists

One of the common separating functions of the **comma** concerns lists. The individual items in a list of three or more items are separated by commas. Whether a comma is put before the word *and* which follows the second-last item is now a matter of choice. Some people dislike the use of the comma in this situation, sometimes called the **Oxford comma** or **serial comma**, and, indeed, it was formerly considered wrong. However, it has become very common in **British English** and is even more common in **American English**. It is best to insert such a comma if there is any possibility of confusion arising from its omission.

In the following sentences the underlined words form lists containing commas:

At the sports club we can play *tennis, squash, badminton and table tennis*.
We need to buy *bread, milk, fruit and sugar*.
They are *studying French, German, Spanish and Russian*.
We *opened the door, let ourselves in, fed the cat and started to cook a meal*.

The comma as a separating device in a list of adjectives

In cases where there is a list of adjectives before a noun, the use of commas between the adjectives is now optional although it was formerly standard practice. Thus the sentences

She wore a long, red, sequinned dress.
and
She wore a long red sequinned dress.

are both considered correct these days. When the adjective immediately before the noun has a closer relationship with it than the other adjectives, and indeed often helps to define the noun, no comma should be used before that adjective, as in the sentences

We want to buy some large juicy green peppers.
and
They live in a beautiful old fishing village.

It would be quite wrong to place a comma before the

word *green* in the first sentence or before the word *fishing* in the second sentence.

> **NB: Last item in a list**
>
> Confusion may arise if the last item in the list contains the word *and* used in its own right as an essential part of the sentence, as in:
>
> *In the pub they served ham salad, shepherd's pie, omelette, and pie and chips*.
>
> In such cases it as well to put a comma before the final connecting *and* to avoid confusion.
>
> If the list of items is a very long one or the items in the list consist of several words a **semi-colon** is sometimes used instead of a **comma** *(see* page 266).

Commas and relative clauses

Commas are not normally used to separate main clauses and **relative clauses** *(see* page 61), where the relative clause is an essential part of the sentence and not an additional piece of information, as in:

The woman whom I met was a friend's sister.

In other words, a **defining relative clause** is not separated from the main clause by a comma.

However, commas are used to separate the main clause from a relative clause which is not required to identify the person or thing that you are talking about, but which is simply giving additional information, as in:

My father, who lived in London, died early last year.

In other words, where a **non-defining relative clause** divides the parts of a main clause the clause is placed within **commas**.

Commas and subordinate clauses

Commas are not now usually used to separate main clauses and **subordinate clauses** (*see* page 54) as in:

He left when we arrived
and
They came to the party although we didn't expect them to.

However, if the subordinate clause precedes the main clause, it is sometimes followed by a comma. This is especially true if it is a reasonably long clause, as in:

Although we stopped and thought about it for quite a long time, we still made the wrong decision.

If the clause is quite short, a comma is not usually inserted, as in:

Although it rained we had a good holiday.
and
If you go you will regret it.

The **comma** is <u>never</u> used to separate a main clause from a clause beginning with *that*, as in *I knew very well that I was right*.

However, as is the case with all lists, **commas** are used to separate clauses beginning with *that* if there are several of them, as in:

Police know that the bankrobbers were armed, that they wore balaclavas to conceal their faces, that they were all of medium height and that they escaped in a blue transit van.

NB: To avoid confusion
It is important to insert a **comma** between a **subordinate clause** and a main clause if doing so prevents any possibility of confusion.

For example, confusion can arise when a subordinate clause ends with a verb and the following clause begins with a noun, as in:

After the pupils had finished reading, the books were returned to the school library.

Here the use of the comma is an aid to clarity. Otherwise you could read the first part of the sentence as *After the pupils had finished reading the books ...*

The comma as a separating device in clauses joined by coordinating conjunctions

A **comma** may be used to separate main clauses joined by a **coordinating conjunction** (*see* page 217) but this is not usual if the clauses have the same subject and the coordinating conjunction is *and*, as in *She swept the floor and dusted the table*.

In cases where the subjects are different and the clauses are fairly long, it is best to insert a comma, as in *They took with them all the furniture and appliances and anything of any value, and she was left with nothing*.

When the coordinating conjunction is *but,* the use of a comma to mark off the main clause is more a matter of choice, especially when both clauses are quite long.

NB: To avoid repetition
A comma can be inserted to avoid repeating a verb in the second of two clauses, as in:

He plays golf and tennis, his brother rugby.

The comma as separating device with initial phrases

A **comma** is often used to separate an **adverb** or an **adverbial phrase** at the beginning of a sentence from the rest of the sentence, as with *However* in:

The weather was not great and it rained a lot. However, we had an interesting and enjoyable holiday.

Nowadays, the use of a **comma** in such situations is sometimes considered optional. However, it is essential to insert a comma if there is any possibility of confusion.

For example, in the sentence

Normally, intelligent students will attend their lectures on a regular basis.

the meaning is changed slightly by the omission of the comma. The longer the expression is, the more likely it is to need a **comma** after it, as in:

After a great deal of consideration, I decided to accept the invitation.

The comma with terms of address

Commas are always used to separate **terms of address** from the rest of the sentence, as in the following sentences:

Mary, I'm afraid I have some bad news for you about your proposed holiday.
Please come this way, Mrs Brown.
Thanks a lot, John.
Now, ladies, what can I get you?
Right, James, I'm ready to leave now.
Doctor Jones, I have an important call for you.

The comma with tag questions

The **comma** is used to separate a **tag question** (*see* page 37) from the rest of a sentence, as in the following sentences:

It's a beautiful day, isn't it?
You do love him, don't you?
He still smokes, doesn't he?
She's not happy, is she?
We can still go, can't we?
They've won again, haven't they?
It isn't raining again, is it?

The comma with interjections

The **comma** is used to separate an **interjection** from the rest of a sentence, as in the following sentences:

Look, there's the train coming.
Heavens, I've never seen such heavy rain!
Wait, she's here now!
Gosh, I'm going to be late!

The comma used in pairs as a means of separation or parenthesis

The **comma** is used in pairs to separate phrases or words that are naturally cut off from the main sense of the rest of the sentence, as if they were additional thoughts or qualifications to what is being said in the rest of the sentence, as in:

The project was, on the whole, successful.

In such a sentence the clause within the commas can be removed without altering the basic meaning. In this respect the use of a pair of commas resembles the use of **brackets** (*see* page 259).

The underlined expressions in the following sentences illustrate this use of the **comma**:

Jim, <u>sensible as ever,</u> told them both to talk things over.
My first impression of him, <u>to be honest,</u> was not very favourable.
We realized, <u>nevertheless,</u> that we could still face problems.
I knew, <u>of course,</u> that something might still go wrong.
I knew all too well, <u>in fact,</u> that he was not telling the truth.

NB: Use both commas
Care should be taken to include both commas. It is easy to forget to include the second one of the pair.

The comma with nouns or phrases in apposition

A noun or noun phrase is said to be **in apposition** when it is placed next to another noun or noun phrase and provides further information about it, especially by saying something that identifies or describes them. In such a situation, the main noun or phrase and the amplifying noun or phrase refer to the same person or thing.

When such a noun or noun phrase is placed after the main noun or noun phrase in the sentence, a comma is almost always placed after the main noun or noun phrase to separate it from the amplifying noun or noun phrase, as in:

Dan Jones, the well-known racing driver, has been involved in a serious car accident.

However, when the amplifying noun or noun phrase is placed before the main noun or noun phrase it is now usual to omit the comma between them when the noun phrases involved are very short, as in:

My son Mike lives with us.
and
The singer Joan Green gave a short recital.

When the noun phrases involved are quite long, it is best to include the comma, as in:

The person who suggested the scheme, Jim Blunt, has now left the company.

In the following sentences the underlined words are in **apposition**:

Jack Blair, <u>our managing director,</u> has resigned.

Sue Brown, <u>leader of the protest campaign,</u> has given a statement to the press.

Peter Shaw, <u>my cousin's husband,</u> is representing the family.

Mike Black, <u>our local Labour MP,</u> has stated his opposition to the scheme.

The head of the local primary school, <u>Jane Lewis,</u> is very much in favour of improved sports facilities.

My elder brother's latest girlfriend, <u>Liz Grant,</u> is quite a famous fashion model.

The writer <u>Lou Wilson</u> is giving a talk at the local bookshop tonight.

Her husband <u>Pete</u> is a very nice man.

The comma and numbers

A **comma** is used when writing a number that is made up of four or more figures, as in:

£45,000
12,000 kilometres
1,000.

However, this is not the case with a date, as in:

1066
1984.

EXERCISES 8

Insert **commas** where this is appropriate in the following passages.

1

Mary's son Mark is a brilliant linguist and works as an interpreter. He speaks fluent French German Spanish and Russian and has a good knowledge of Danish Norwegian and Swedish. His wife Maria who is Spanish used to teach at the local senior school before the birth of the first of their four children. John Brown the head teacher there says that she was an excellent teacher and he would like her to go back to work.

Maria loves teaching and of course would like to get her old job back. Sadly the cost of childcare in the area is extremely expensive. In addition Mark has to travel a lot in connection with his work and cannot help much with looking after the children. Mark caring as ever would like to help more and spend more time with the children but this is simply not possible.

Maria's mother who lives with them is too frail to take care of four active children and so Maria will have to postpone going back to work for a while. She sometimes talks about taking on some private pupils who are in need of special tutoring to help them pass their exams. This on the whole sounds like a very good idea.

2

'Please sit down here Mr Smith. Dr Black will see you next. Mrs Wilson Dr Jones will see you now. Can you manage

all right? It's so difficult to walk on crutches until you get used to them isn't it? Still your leg seems to be healing nicely doesn't it? Ms Black Dr Martin is off ill. I've given you an appointment with Dr Blair who's acting as a locum while Dr Martin is off. I hope your cold is a bit better. This cold weather's doesn't help does it? Look it's started snowing. Take care Mrs Wilson! The pavements may be quite slippery and you certainly don't want to fall again do you?'

3

We've just started a literary society in the village and we've already got quite a few members. My aunt who has just moved here is the president of the society and I am the secretary. It involves more work than I thought it would but nevertheless I am enjoying it.

Sometimes we invite a speaker to address the society sometimes one of the society members gives a talk and sometimes we just have an informal discussion. There are several people among the members who have worked in publishing and we also have some members who are professional writers. For example Bill Jackson the society's treasurer is quite a well-known travel writer and his wife Jean Jackson who writes under the pseudonym Jenny Adams is making quite a name for herself as a crime writer.

Alas we have been unable to persuade Mark Hill writer of several very successful novels about espionage to join the society. He says that he is too busy with his writing and in addition he travels a lot. Still we have quite enough members to have a successful society.

1

Mary's son Mark is a brilliant linguist and works as an interpreter. He speaks fluent French, German, Spanish and Russian and has a good knowledge of Danish, Norwegian and Swedish. His wife Maria, who is Spanish, used to teach at the local senior school before the birth of the first of their four children. John Brown, the head teacher there, says that she was an excellent teacher and he would like her to go back to work.

Maria loves teaching and, of course, would like to get her old job back. Sadly, the cost of childcare in the area is extremely expensive. In addition, Mark has to travel a lot in connection with his work and cannot help much with looking after the children. Mark, caring as ever, would like to help more and spend more time with the children, but this is simply not possible.

Maria's mother, who lives with them, is too frail to take care of four active children and so Maria will have to postpone going back to work for a while. She sometimes talks about taking on some private pupils who are in need of special tutoring to help them pass their exams. This, on the whole, sounds like a very good idea.

2

'Please sit down here, Mr Smith. Dr Black will see you next. Mrs Wilson, Dr Jones will see you now. Can you manage all right? It's so difficult to walk on crutches until you get used to them, isn't it? Still, your leg seems

to be healing nicely, doesn't it? Ms Black, Dr Martin is off ill. I've given you an appointment with Dr Blair who's acting as a locum while Dr Martin is off. I hope your cold is a bit better. This cold weather's doesn't help, does it? Look, it's started snowing. Take care, Mrs Wilson! The pavements may be quite slippery and you certainly don't want to fall again, do you?'

3

We've just started a literary society in the village and we've already got quite a few members. My aunt, who has just moved here, is the president of the society and I am the secretary. It involves more work than I thought it would, but, nevertheless, I am enjoying it.

Sometimes we invite a speaker to address the society, sometimes one of the society members gives a talk and sometimes we just have an informal discussion. There are several people among the members who have worked in publishing and we also have some members who are pro-fessional writers. For example, Bill Jackson, the society's treasurer, is quite a well-known travel writer and his wife Jean Jackson, who writes under the pseudonym Jenny Adams, is making quite a name for herself as a crime writer.

Alas, we have been unable to persuade Mark Hill, writer of several very successful novels about espionage, to join the society. He says that he is too busy with his writing and, in addition, he travels a lot. Still, we have quite enough members to have a successful society.

Brackets

Brackets, in common with a pair of **commas** or a pair of **dashes** (*see* page 263), are used to enclose information that is in some way additional to a main statement. The information so enclosed is said to be **in parenthesis** and the pair of brackets enclosing it can be known as **parentheses**. The information that is enclosed in the brackets is purely supplementary or explanatory in nature and could be removed without changing the overall basic meaning or grammatical completeness of the statement.

Brackets, like **commas** and **dashes**, interrupt the flow of the main statement but **brackets** indicate a more definite or clear-cut interruption. The fact that they are more visually obvious emphasizes this. Material within **brackets** can be **one word**, as in the following sentences:

In a local wine bar we had some delicious crepes (pancakes)
and
They didn't have the chutzpah (nerve) to challenge her.

Material within **brackets** can also take the form of **dates**, as in the following sentences:

Robert Louis Stevenson (1850–94) wrote Treasure Island.
and
Animal Farm *was written by George Orwell (1903–50).*

The material within **brackets** can also take the form of a **phrase**, as in the following sentences:

They served lasagne (a kind of pasta) and some delicious veal.
and
They were drinking Calvados (a kind of brandy made from apples).

The material within **brackets** can also take the form of a **clause**, as in the following sentences:

We were to have supper (or so they called it) later in the evening.
and
They went for a walk round the loch (as a lake is called in Scotland) before taking their departure.

The material within **brackets** can also take the form of a **complete sentence**, as in the following sentences:

He was determined (we don't know why) to tackle the problem alone.
and
She made it clear (nothing could be more clear) that she was not interested in the offer.

Sentences that appear in brackets in the middle of a sentence are not usually given an initial capital letter or a full stop, as in the following sentence:

They very much desired (she had no idea why) to purchase her house.

If the material within **brackets** comes at the end of a sentence the full stop comes outside the second bracket, as in the following sentence:

For some reason we agreed to visit her at home (we had no idea where she lived).

If the material in **brackets** is a sentence which comes between two other sentences it is treated like a normal sentence with an initial capital letter and a closing full stop, as in the following sentences:

He never seems to do any studying. (He is always either asleep or watching television.) Still, he does brilliantly in his exams.

Punctuation of the main statement is unaffected by the presence of the brackets and their enclosed material, except that any punctuation that would have followed the word before the first bracket follows the second bracket, as in the following sentence:

He lives in London (I am not sure exactly where), though his family live in France.

There are various shapes of brackets. **Round brackets** are the most common type. **Square brackets** are sometimes used to enclose information that is contained inside other information already in brackets, as in the following sentence:

(Christopher Marlowe [1564–93] was a contemporary of Shakespeare).

Square brackets are also sometimes used to enclose information that is contained in a piece of writing where round brackets have already been used for some other purpose. Thus, in a dictionary if round brackets are used to separate off the pronunciation, square brackets are sometimes used to separate off the etymologies.

Square brackets are also used for editorial comments in a scholarly work where the material within brackets consists of an editorial comment or expanation within a quotation by another author. They can also be used in scholarly writing to indicate words or phrases that have been altered by the author in a quotation by another writer.

Dash

The **dash**, written as — (**em dash**, used close up to text) or – (**en dash**, with a space on either side), takes the form of a short line, resembling an extended **hyphen** (-). The dash indicates a short break in the continuity of a sentence or it is used to extend a sentence. It often serves the same purpose as **brackets** except that it is usually considered to be much less formal. The **dash** fulfils various functions, as explained below.

The **dash** can be used to emphasize a word or phrase, as in:

They parted company then—forever.

The **dash** can also be used to add a remark to the end of a sentence, as in:

They had no money at the end of the month—a regular state of affairs with this extravagant couple.

The **dash** can also be used to introduce a statement that adds to or explains what has been said, as in:

The burglar took everything of value—paintings, jewellery, silverware and several thousand pounds in money.

The **dash** can also be used as a linking device to sum up what has gone before, as in:

Famine, drought, disease—these are the seemingly insuperable problems that the villagers are facing.

The **dash** can also be used to introduce an afterthought, as in:

You can come with me if you like—I'd appreciate your company.

The **dash** can also be used to introduce a sharp change of subject, as in:

I'll be with you in a minute—what was that noise?

The **dash** can also be used to introduce some kind of balance in a sentence, as in:

It's going to take at least three of you to get this heavy table out of here—one at each end to carry it and one to hold the door open.

The **dash** is sometimes found as part of a pair. A pair of dashes can act in a similar way to a pair of round **brackets** (*see* page 260). They can be used to indicate a break in continuity in a sentence, as in:

We prayed—prayed as we had never done before—that the children would be safe.
and (showing a spaced **en dash**)
We came to the conclusion – after due consideration – that we had done the wrong thing.

NB: Don't forget
When using a pair of dashes as a substitute for a pair of brackets do not forget to include the second dash. Its omission is a common fault.

The **dash** is also used to indicate a hesitation in speech, as in:

I don't think—well—maybe—you could be right.

The **dash** can also be used to indicate the omission of part of a word or name, as in:

The witness, who is being referred to by police simply as Mrs D—, has not yet come forward
and
It's none of your d— business.

In this last sentence *d—* is short for *damned* as a way of not writing a swear word in full. The **asterisk** (*see* page 295) is often used in this way.

The **en dash** can also be used as a replacement for the word *to*, as a connection between points in time or places, as in:

1850–1900 and *London–Paris.*

> ### NB: Dashes—don't overuse
> Be careful not to overuse the dash, especially in more formal pieces of writing. It is tempting to do so when another thought occurs to you as you write, but you can end up with rather an unattractive page peppered with these.

Semicolon

The semicolon as a link

The **semicolon** (;) is a rather formal form of punctuation. It is mainly used between clauses that are not joined by any form of conjunction, as in:

We had a wonderful holiday; sadly they did not.
and
He was a marvellous friend; he is much missed.

The part before the **semicolon** and the part after could both be sentences in their own right. The **semicolon** is used to show a closer link between the two parts of the sentence. It has the force of a strong comma. A **dash** (*see* page 263) is sometimes used instead.

The semicolon as a separation device in lists

The **semicolon** is also used to separate the items in a long list or series of things so that the said list seems less complex and easier to understand, as in:

The young man who wants to be a journalist has applied everywhere. He has applied to The Times *in London;* The Globe *and* Mail *in Toronto;* The Age *in Melbourne;* The Tribune *in Chicago.*

It is also used in lists in which the individual items are quite long, as in:

We tried various ways to raise money. We approached the local bank manger; we asked the local council for a grant; we approached local businessmen for a contribution; and we organized various charity events.

The use of a **semicolon** in this situation resembles that of the **comma** (*see* page 244), especially a particularly strong comma, except that the **semicolon** is more formal and it is more common in more complicated lists.

The semicolon as separation device in lists of word groups already containing commas

The **semicolon** is also used to separate items in a list which already contains a number of commas in the individual items in the list, as in:

Those guests present at the wedding included Mr and Mrs Brown and their daughters Mary, Jane and Sue; Mr and Mrs Lewis and their sons Tom, Frank and Jack; Miss Taylor and her nieces Liz, Carol and Meg; Ken, Mike and Mark Greene.

To use yet more commas to separate the list of items would cause confusion. Thus, the **semicolon** is used in such a context in the interests of clarity.

The semicolon as a separation device before certain adverbs

The **semicolon** is also sometimes used before such **adverbs** as *however, nevertheless, hence, moreover* and *furthermore* in such situations where a preceding pause is required but a pause that is longer and stronger than that which can be provided by a **comma**, as in:

We have extra seats for the concert; however you must decide right now whether you want them or not.
and
Your notice to quit takes effect immediately; furthermore, you will be escorted from the building and your personal belongings from your desk will be sent on to you.

Colon

The colon as a separating device in a two-part sentence

The **colon** (:) is a punctuation mark that is used to separate two parts of a sentence when the first leads on to the second. The **colon** is used to explain, interpret, clarify or amplify what has gone before it, as in:

The standard of school work here is extremely high: it is almost university standard.
and
The fuel bills are giving cause for concern: they are almost double last year's.
and
We have some new information: the allies have landed.

The colon as a linking device or introduction

The **colon** is used to introduce a list, as in:

The recipe says we need: tomatoes, peppers, courgettes, garlic, oregano and basil.
and
The boy has a huge list of things he needs for school: blazer, trousers, shirts, sweater, ties, shoes, tennis shoes, rugby boots, sports clothes and leisure wear.

The **colon** is also used to introduce a quotation or a piece of direct speech, as in:

One of his favourite quotations was: 'If music be the food of love, play on'.
and
The headmaster strode on to the platform, looking solemnly at the assembled students, and his statement was concise: 'I will not allow this kind of behaviour in my school.'

The **colon** is sometimes used with numerals in references to the time of day, the date and ratios, as in:

7:30 a.m. and *22:11:72* and *7:3.*

The **colon** is often used in the titles of books, for example where there is a subtitle or explanatory title, as in *The Dark Years: the Economy in the 1930s.*

In informal writing, the **dash** is sometimes used instead of the **colon**. Indeed the dash tends to be overused for this purpose.

EXERCISES 9

1 Rewrite the following sentences, inserting **brackets** or a **bracket** where this is appropriate.

a *In the French restaurant we had ragout (actually just a stew, but tasting nicer than any stew I've ever had.*

b *We had quite a lot of wine with dinner and afterwards we had Armagnac a kind of French brandy).*

c *We arranged to meet in the large square (the Italians call it a piazza in the centre of the town.*

d *They say that they are planning to visit us in the fall as the Americans call autumn.*

e *He went away quite suddenly no one knows where or why) some years ago and has not been in touch with his family since.*

f *Both Oliver Twist and Bleak House were written by Charles Dickens 1812–70.*

g *(Vincent Van Gogh [1853–90 is one of Holland's most well-known painters.*

2 Rewrite the following sentences, inserting a **dash** or a **pair of dashes** where this is appropriate.

a *You can come to the dinner as my partner I'd like that very much.*

b *I'm just going now what did I do with my car keys?*

c *The drunk driver said to the police that where he was going was none of their d   business.*

d *We begged our captors begged them on bended knee to release us.*

e *Christopher Marlowe (1564 93) was a contemporary of Shakespeare.*

f *Wealth, power, status these were the things which he craved all his life and totally failed to achieve.*

g *We were awoken at dawn by the noisy barking of the dog next door a regular occurrence these days.*

h *I'm just about to serve dinner was that the doorbell?*

3 Rewrite the following sentences, inserting a **semi-colon** where this is appropriate.

a *Their best player has moved to another team he will be greatly missed.*

b *We did our very best to save the old building from demolition. We sent a letter of protest to the council we sought the help of our local MP we launched a protest campaign we collected hundreds of signatures from fellow objectors and we held demonstrations outside the town hall.*

c *The members of the choir had all practised very hard before the competition sadly they came last.*

d *We visited many historical sites in Britain. We went to the Tower of London the Houses of Parliament in London some of the colleges at Oxford Durham Cathedral the historical cities of Chester and York.*

4
Rewrite the following sentences, inserting a **colon** where this is appropriate.

a *Economists are worried about house prices they are falling rapidly.*

b *I've packed a picnic lunch for us French bread, cheese, tomatoes, salad, grapes, apples, chocolate, white wine and mineral water. Can you think of anything else?*

c *They have just released the name of the new head teacher James Hunt, presently the deputy head.*

d *The title of the book is The Years of Conflict a Reassessment of the Two World Wars.*

ANSWERS 9

1

a *In the French restaurant we had ragout (actually just a stew, but tasting nicer than any stew I've ever had).*

b *We had quite a lot of wine with dinner and afterwards we had Armagnac (a kind of French brandy).*

c *We arranged to meet in the large square (the Italians call it a piazza) in the centre of the town.*

d *They say that they are planning to visit us in the fall (as the Americans call autumn).*

e *He went away quite suddenly (no one knows where or why) some years ago and has not been in touch with his family since.*

f *Both Oliver Twist and Bleak House were written by Charles Dickens (1812–70).*

g *(Vincent van Gogh [1853–90] is one of Holland's most well-known painters.)*

2

a *You can come to the dinner as my partner—I'd like that very much.*

b *I'm just going now—what did I do with my car keys?*

c *The drunk driver said to the police that where he was going was none of their d— business.*

d *We begged our captors—begged them on bended knee—to release us.*

e *Christopher Marlowe (1564–93) was a contemporary of Shakespeare.*

f *Wealth, power, status—these were the things which he craved all his life and totally failed to achieve.*

g *We were awoken at dawn by the noisy barking of the dog next door—a regular occurrence these days.*

h *I'm just about to serve dinner—was that the doorbell?*

3

a *Their best player has moved to another team; he will be greatly missed.*

b *We did our very best to save the old building from demolition. We sent a letter of protest to the council; we sought the help of our local MP; we launched a protest* campaign; we collected hundreds of signatures from fellow objectors; and we held demonstrations outside the town hall.

c *The members of the choir had all practised very hard before the competition; sadly they came last.*

d *We visited many historical sites in Britain. We went to the Tower of London; the Houses of Parliament in London; some of the colleges at Oxford; Durham Cathedral; the historical cities of Chester and York.*

4

a *Economists are worried about house prices: they are falling rapidly.*

b *I've packed a picnic lunch for us: French bread, cheese, tomatoes, salad, grapes, apples, chocolate, white wine and mineral water. Can you think of anything else?*

c *They have just released the name of the new head teacher: James Hunt, presently the deputy head.*

d *The title of the book is* The Years of Conflict: a Reassessment of the Two World Wars.

Hyphen

A **hyphen** (-) is used to join two words together or to indicate that a word has been broken at the end of a line because of lack of space. It is used in a variety of situations.

The **hyphen** is used as the prefixed element in a proper noun, as in *pre-Christian, post-Renaissance, anti-British, anti-Semitic, pro-French* and *pro-American*.

The **hyphen** is also used in this way before dates or numbers, as in *pre-1914, pre-1066, post-1920, post-1745*.

It is also used in this way before abbreviations such as *pro-BBC, anti-EU* and *anti-TUC*.

The **hyphen** is sometimes used for clarification and to avoid confusion. Some words are ambiguous without the presence of a hyphen. For example, *re-cover*, as in *re-cover a chair*, is spelt with a hyphen to differentiate it from *recover*, as in *The accident victim is likely to recover*. Similarly, it is used in *re-form*, meaning 'to form again', as in *They have decided to re-form the society which closed last year* to differentiate the word from *reform*, meaning 'to improve, to become better behaved', as in *He was wild as a young man but he has reformed now*.

The **hyphen** was formerly used to separate a prefix from the main element of a word if the main element begins with a vowel, as in *pre-eminent*, but there is a growing tendency in modern usage to omit the hyphen in such cases. At the moment both *pre-eminent* and *preeminent* are found.

However, if the omission of the hyphen results in double *i*, the hyphen is usually retained, as in *anti-inflationary* and *semi-insulated*.

The **hyphen** was formerly used in words formed with the prefix *non-*, such as *non-functional, non-political, non-flammable* and *non-pollutant*.

However, there is a growing tendency to omit the hyphen in such cases, as in *nonfunctional* and *nonpollutant*. At the moment both forms of such words are common.

The **hyphen** is usually used with the prefix *ex-* in the sense of 'former', as in *ex-wife* and *ex-president*.

The **hyphen** is usually used when *self-* is prefixed to words, such as *self-styled*, *self-starter* and *self-evident*.

Use or non-use of the **hyphen** is often a matter of choice, house style of a particular organization, or frequency of usage, as in *drawing-room* or *drawing room*, and *dining-room* or *dining room*.

There is a modern tendency to punctuate more lightly than was formerly the case and so, in modern usage, use of the hyphen in such expressions is less frequent.

The **hyphen** is always used in some fixed compounds of two or three words or more, such as *son-in-law, good-for-nothing* and *devil-may-care*.

NB: To include or omit?
The length of compounds often affects the inclusion or omission of the **hyphen**.

Compounds of two short elements that are well-established words tend not to be hyphenated, as in:

bedroom and *toothbrush*.

Compound words with longer elements are more likely to be hyphenated, as in:

engine-driver and *carpet-layer*.

The **hyphen** is sometimes used in some compounds formed from **phrasal verbs** (*see* page 73) and sometimes not. Thus both *take-over* and *takeover* are common, and *run-up* and *runup* are both common. Again the use of the hyphen is a matter of choice.

However, some words formed from phrasal verbs are usually spelt without a hyphen, as in *breakthrough*.

The **hyphen** is usually used in compound adjectives consisting of two elements, the second of which ends in *-ed*, such as *heavy-hearted, fair-haired, fair-minded* and *long-legged*.

The **hyphen** is usually used in compound adjectives when they are used before nouns, such as *gas-fired central heating, oil-based paints, solar-heated buildings* and *chocolate-coated biscuits*.

The **hyphen** is usually used in compounds containing certain adverbs, sometimes to avoid ambiguity, as in *his best-known opera*, *an ill-considered venture* and *a half-planned scheme*.

The **hyphen** is generally not used in adjectives and participles preceded by an adverb if the adverb ends in -*ly*, as in *a highly talented singer*, *neatly pressed clothes* and *beautifully dressed young women*.

The **hyphen** is used in compound numerals from 21 to 99 when they are written in full, as in *thirty-five gallons, forty-four years, sixty-seven miles* and *two hundred and forty-five miles*. Compound numbers such as *three hundred* and *two thousand* are not hyphenated.

The **hyphen** is used in fractions, such as *three-quarters, two-thirds* and *seven-eighths*.

The **hyphen** is also used in such number phrases as *a seventeenth-century play, a sixteenth-century church, a five-gallon bucket, a five-year contract* and *a third-year student*.

> **NB: Repeated hyphenated elements**
> In the case of two or more compound hyphenated adjectives with the same second element qualifying the same noun, the common element need not be repeated but the **hyphen** should be, as in *two- and three-bedroom houses* and *long- and short-haired dogs*.

The hyphen in word-breaks

The other use of **hyphens** is to break words at the ends of lines. Formerly, people were more careful about where they broke words. Previously, words were broken up according to etymological principles, but there is a growing tendency to break words according to how they are pronounced or just where it seems convenient.

Some dictionaries or spelling dictionaries give help with the division and hyphenation of individual words and, if you are in doubt, you should consult one of these.

NB: Where to break

Generally speaking, one-syllable words should not be divided and words should not be broken after the first letter of a word or before the last letter.

Also, care should be taken not to break up words, for example by forming elements that are words in their own right, in such a way as to mislead the reader. Thus divisions such as 'the-rapist' and 'mans-laughter' should be avoided.

Rewrite the following sentences, inserting a **hyphen** where this is appropriate.

1 *The candidate is very proBritish and incredibly antiEuropean.*
2 *The remains are known to be preChristian.*
3 *There were a great many elegantly dressed women at the wedding.*
4 *He is an excellent after dinner speaker and is in much demand.*
5 *He was the most highly qualified and talented of all the candidates for the post.*
6 *We are seeking a strict, but fair minded, judge for the talent competition.*
7 *The child is using water based paints.*
8 *We have a gas fired central heating system.*
9 *The glass is two thirds full.*
10 *It was a distance of three hundred miles.*
11 *They walked forty five miles across a bleak terrain.*
12 *There are still two and three bedroom flats for sale in the complex.*
13 *The vase cost two hundred and fifty five pounds.*
14 *The previous manager had a very heavy handed approach to dealing with employees' problems.*
15 *It is a rough haired breed of dog.*
16 *He is a good for nothing who has never done a day's work in his life.*
17 *Red haired girls often look marvellous in green.*

18 *I think I'll have one of those cream covered cakes.*
19 *Fair skinned people burn easily in the sun.*
20 *Her father in law has just died and she is helping with the funeral arrangements.*
21 *He gave a lecture to second year students.*
22 *The sixteenth century church in the village is badly in need of repair.*
23 *The members of the hotel staff are always immaculately dressed.*
24 *We are currently putting together a five year plan for the company.*
25 *She is two thirds of the way through her art course.*

ANSWERS 10

1 *The candidate is very pro-British and incredibly anti-European.*
2 *The remains are known to be pre-Christian.*
3 *There were a great many elegantly dressed women at the wedding.*
4 *He is an excellent after-dinner speaker and is in much demand.*
5 *He was the most highly qualified and talented of all the candidates for the post.*
6 *We are seeking a strict, but fair-minded, judge for the talent competition.*
7 *The child is using water-based paints.*
8 *We have a gas-fired central heating system.*
9 *The glass is two-thirds full.*

10 *It was a distance of three hundred miles.*

11 *They walked forty-five miles across a bleak terrain.*

12 *There are still two- and three-bedroom flats for sale in the complex.*

13 *The vase cost two hundred and fifty-five pounds.*

14 *The previous manager had a very heavy-handed approach to dealing with employees' problems.*

15 *It is a rough-haired breed of dog.*

16 *He is a good-for-nothing who has never done a day's work in his life.*

17 *Red-haired girls often look marvellous in green.*

18 *I think I'll have one of those cream-covered cakes.*

19 *Fair-skinned people burn easily in the sun.*

20 *Her father-in-law has just died and she is helping with the funeral arrangements.*

21 *He gave a lecture to second-year students.*

22 *The sixteenth-century church in the village is badly in need of repair.*

23 *The members of the hotel staff are always immaculately dressed.*

24 *We are currently putting together a five-year plan for the company.*

25 *She is two-thirds of the way through her art course.*

Quotation marks

Quotation marks and direct speech

Quotation marks ('. . .' or ". . ."), also known as **inverted commas**, are used to enclose material that is part of **direct speech**. **Direct speech** is a term used to describe the reporting of speech by repeating exactly the actual words used by the speaker, as in the following example:

Peter said, 'I am tired of this.'

'I am tired of this.' is a piece of **direct speech**. Similarly in the following example:

Jane asked, 'Where are you going?'

'Where are you going?' is a piece of **direct speech**.

Quotation marks are used at the beginning and end of pieces of **direct speech**. Only the words actually spoken are placed within the quotation marks, as in *'If I were you,' he said, 'I would refuse to go.'*

The **quotation marks** involved can be either **single** ('. . .') or **double** (". . .") according to preference or house style. Be sure to be consistent in your use of either single or double **quotation marks**.

If there is a statement such as *he said* following the piece of **direct speech**, a **comma** is placed before the **second** inverted comma, as in *'Come along,' he said*.

If the piece of direct speech is a **question** or **exclamation**, a **question mark** or **exclamation mark** is put instead of the **comma**, as in:

'What are you doing?' asked John
and
'Get away from me!' she screamed.

If a statement such as *he said* is placed within a sentence in **direct speech**, a **comma** is placed after *he said* and the second part of the piece of direct speech does *not* begin with a capital letter, as in:

'I know very well,' he said, 'that you do not like me.'

If the piece of **direct speech** includes a complete sentence, the sentence begins with a **capital letter**, as in:

'I am going away,' she said, 'and I am not coming back. Really, I don't feel that I belong here anymore.'

NB: Before or after?
The full stop at the end of a piece of direct speech that is a sentence should go before the closing inverted comma.

Quotation marks and paragraphs

If the piece of **direct speech** quoted takes up more than one **paragraph** (*see* page 44), **quotation marks** are placed at the beginning of each new **paragraph**.

However, **quotation marks** are not placed at the end of each **paragraph**, just at the end of the final one.

Quotation marks and dialogue

When writing a story, etc, that includes dialogue or conversation, each new piece of direct speech should begin on a new line or sometimes in a new paragraph.

Other uses of quotation marks

Quotation marks are not used only to indicate direct speech. They have other uses.

Quotation marks and titles

Quotation marks are sometimes used to indicate the title of a book or newspaper. The **quotation marks** used in this way can be either **single** or **double**, according to individual preference or according to the house style of a particular organization.

If a piece of direct speech contains the title of a book, newspaper, poem, song, etc, it should be put in the opposite type of quotation marks to those used to enclose the piece of direct speech. Thus, if **single quotation marks** have been used in the **direct speech**, then **double quotation marks** should be used for the **title** within the direct speech, as in:

'Have you read "Animal Farm" by George Orwell?' the teacher asked.

If **double quotation marks** have been used for the **direct speech**, **single quotation marks** should be used for the **title**, as in:

"Have you read 'Animal Farm' by George Orwell?" the teacher asked.

Quotation marks and a direct quotation

When a piece of writing includes a **direct quotation** from another book, piece of text, or speaker, the words which are quoted are contained within quotation marks, either single or double, according to individual preference or house style, as in:

In his report the marketing director refers to the new product as 'a technological miracle'.
and
In his autobiography Brian refers to that part of his life as 'a terrible living nightmare' and his sister confirms that that was the case.

If the quotation from another piece of text or speaker is fairly long it is often set out below on the page and indented without quotation marks, as in:

The victim of the attack gave the following statement to the police:

> *It was pitch dark and I was attacked from behind. I had no opportunity to see my assailant and, therefore, I could not possibly identify him, if, indeed, it*

was a man. I suppose it could have been a woman. At any rate, I was hit over the head by something heavy and I knew nothing more till I woke up lying on the ground with a very sore head. My wallet and watch had gone.

Sometimes writers use **quotation marks** round a word or words to indicate that this expression is not their own or not one that they would have chosen to use, as in:

The 'exclusive hotel' we stayed in was far from comfortable.

Sometimes the word *so-called* is also included, as in:

The so-called 'exclusive hotel' we stayed in was far from comfortable.

However, either the quotation marks or the word *so-called* will suffice on their own. You do not need to use both.

NB: Titles
Often, **titles** are put in **italic type** instead of **quotation marks**. This avoids the clumsiness that can occur when both sets of quotation marks end on the same word, as in

The pupil replied, 'No, I have not read *Animal Farm*.'

1 Rewrite the following conversations, inserting **quotation marks** where this is appropriate.

a
What time is it? asked Mike.
It's nearly 11 o'clock, replied John.
I'd better leave soon, said Mike, because I don't want to be too late home.
If you leave now, said Bill, you'll be in time to catch the last bus.
Good idea! exclaimed Mike, getting up to leave.

b
Mary said, I know that I can't really afford a new dress, but I don't have anything suitable to wear to Sally's wedding.
I bought a new outfit for my cousin's wedding earlier this year, said Lucy, and I've not worn it since. You are welcome to borrow it if you want.
That's very kind of you, said Mary, and we're much the same size. Could I come over to your flat and try it on?
Sure! replied Lucy. Let me know when you want to come. I'll be in most evenings this week.

c
I'm reading Bleak House at the moment. Have you read it? asked Sue.

No, replied Jack, I haven't, but I've read quite a lot of novels by Dickens.
What's your favourite? asked Sue.
I think I like David Copperfield and Hard Times best, said Jack, but I'm fond of A Tale of Two Cities as well. Do you have a favourite, Sue?
Sue replied, Yes, I do. It's Great Expectations, without a doubt.

2 Rewrite the following sentences, inserting **quotation marks** where this is appropriate.

a *The organization's new computer system was hailed by the designers as a triumph for modern technology, but it broke down at least three times a week, on average.*

b *The released hostage described the conditions which he experienced as a hostage as hell on earth.*

c *The so-called home from home turned out to be a damp, cold, run-down cottage in the middle of nowhere.*

d *The accommodation in the exclusive luxury hotel was very basic and the food that was served was appalling and virtually inedible.*

ANSWERS 11

1

a

'What time is it?' asked Mike.

'It's nearly 11 o'clock,' replied John.

'I'd better leave soon,' said Mike, 'because I don't want to be too late home.'

'If you leave now,' said Bill, 'you'll be in time to catch the last bus.'

'Good idea!' exclaimed Mike, getting up to leave.

b

Mary said, 'I know that I can't really afford a new dress, but I don't have anything suitable to wear to Sally's wedding.'

'I bought a new outfit for my cousin's wedding earlier this year,' said Lucy, 'and I've not worn it since. You are welcome to borrow it if you want.'

'That's very kind of you,' said Mary, 'and we're much the same size. Could I come over to your flat and try it on?'

'Sure!' replied Lucy. 'Let me know when you want to come. I'll be in most evenings this week.'

c

'I'm reading "Bleak House" at the moment. Have you read it?' asked Sue.

'No,' replied Jack, 'I haven't, but I've read quite a lot of novels by Dickens.'

'What's your favourite?' asked Sue.

'I think I like "David Copperfield" and "Hard Times" best,' said Jack, 'but I'm fond of "A Tale of Two Cities" as well. Do you have a favourite, Sue?'

Sue replied, 'Yes, I do. It's "Great Expectations", without a doubt.'

2

a The organization's new computer system was hailed by the designers as 'a triumph of modern technology', but it broke down at least three times a week, on average.

b The released hostage described the conditions which he experienced as a hostage as 'hell on earth'.

c The so-called home from home turned out to be a damp, cold, run-down cottage in the middle of nowhere.

d The accommodation in the 'exclusive luxury hotel' was very basic and the food that was served was appalling and virtually inedible.

Other punctuation marks

Apostrophe

An **apostrophe** (') is used with the letter *s* to indicate that something belongs to someone or something. In other words it is used to indicate **possession**.

Many errors centre on the position of the apostrophe in relation to the letter *s*.

A **singular noun** usually indicates possession by adding *'s* (**apostrophe s**) to the singular form as in *the girl's mother, Peter's car, the company's policy, the town's pride and joy*.

A **plural noun** usually indicates possession by adding **s'** (**s apostrophe**) to the plural form ending in *s*, as in *all the teachers' cars, many parents' attitude to discipline*, and by adding *'s* to irregular plural nouns that do not end in *s*, as in *women's shoes*.

In the **possessive form** of a **name** or **singular noun** that ends in *s, x* or *z*, the apostrophe may or may not be followed by *s*. In words of one syllable the final *s* is usually added, as in *James's house, the fox's lair, Roz's dress*.

The final *s* is most frequently omitted in names, particularly in names of three or more syllables, as in *Euripides' plays*. In many cases the presence or absence of the final *s* is a matter of convention.

The **apostrophe** is also used to indicate omitted letters in contracted forms of words, such as *can't* and *you've*.

They are sometimes used to indicate missing century numbers in dates, as the *'60s* and *'70s,* but are not used at the end of decades, etc, as in *1960s,* not *1960's.*

Generally, **apostrophes** are no longer used to indicate omitted letters in shortened forms that are in common use such as *'phone* and *'flu,* now used simply as *phone* and *flu.*

Apostrophes are often omitted **wrongly** in modern usage, particularly in the media and by advertisers, as in *womens hairdressers, childrens helpings.* This is partly because people are unsure about when to use them and when not to use them, and partly because of a modern tendency to punctuate as little as possible.

Apostrophes, on the other hand, are also frequently used **wrongly** nowadays as in *potato's for sale* and *Beware of the dog's.* Again, this is because people are unsure about when, and when not, to use them.

NB: Its and It's

Its is an exception to the possession rule which sometimes causes confusion. When used to indicate possession (*its fault, its engine, its environment*) **its** has no apostrophe.

It is only when used as a contraction that an apostrophe is added (*it's* cold, *it's* raining, *it's still morning*). Similarly, possessive pronouns that end in an *s* never take an apostrophe (*yours, hers, ours, theirs*).

Asterisk

The **asterisk** (*) is commonly used to direct the reader's attention from a particular word or piece of text to a footnote or to another part of the text. The asterisk is placed after the relevant word or piece of text.

The **asterisk** is often used to replace a letter. The **asterisk** is usually one of a series and such a series is often found as a substitute for letters that would make up a word that would cause offence in some way, often swear words, as in:

*I can't open this b****y tin*

The asterisks replace the letters *l o o d*. When the letters are used instead of the asterisks the swear word *bloody* is formed.

Three-dot ellipsis

The **three-dot ellipsis** (...)is used to indicate missing material. This missing material may be one word, as in the sentence

I told you to get the ... out of here

where the missing word is the swear word *hell*.

The missing material may be several words or a longer piece of text. For example, the **three-dot ellipsis** may be used to replace part of a quotation, proverb, etc, as in:

Ah well you know, the moving finger writes ... (where *and, having writ, moves on* is omitted)

and

You know what they say. A stitch in time ... (where *saves nine* is omitted).

It can also be used to indicate an unfinished thought or statement, as in:

We might win handsomely; on the other hand ...

Sometimes a **dash** is used in the above cases.

Oblique

The **oblique** (/) is a diagonal mark that has various uses. Its principal use is to show alternatives, as in:

he/she
Dear Sir/Madam
two-/three-room flat.

The **oblique** is also used in some abbreviations, as in:

c/o Smith (meaning *care of Smith*)

An **oblique** is sometimes used instead of the word *per*, as in:

60km/h (60 kilometres per hour).

EXERCISES 12

1 Rewrite the following sentences, inserting **apostrophes** where this is appropriate.

a *I cant remember his phone number and I dont know his address.*

b *Youll soon find out that youve made the wrong decision.*

c *Wed missed the train and there wasnt another one for several hours.*

d *Its amazing to think that they've known each other since the 60s.*

e *Its an interesting idea, but we need to consider its advantages and disadvantages.*

2 Rewrite the following phrases, inserting an **apostrophe** where this is appropriate.

my mothers house
admiring her new kitchens modern facilities
that streets convenient location
his two aunts wise advice
the only local schools role in the community
that sites most obvious disadvantage
Jacks main objection

mens outdoor clothes
stylish womens hairdressers
a lack of childrens nurseries in the area
Jamess victory over the rest of the competitors
consider all the travel agents best deals
the foxs bushy tail
Rozs beautiful wedding dress
the potatos long-lasting culinary appeal
potatoes for sale here
the last centurys most significant contributions to industry
all vegetables drastically reduced
its universal appeal.

ANSWERS 12

1

a *I can't remember his phone number and I don't know his address.*

b *You'll soon find out that you've made the wrong decision.*

c *We'd missed the train and there wasn't another one for several hours.*

d *It's amazing to think that they've known each other since the '60s.*

e *It's an interesting idea, but we need to consider its advantages and disadvantages.*

2

my mother's house
admiring her new kitchen's modern facilities
that street's convenient location
his two aunts' wise advice
the only local school's role in the community
that site's most obvious disadvantage
Jack's main objection
men's outdoor clothes
stylish women's hairdressers
a lack of children's nurseries in the area
James's victory over the rest of the competitors
consider all the travel agents' best deals
the fox's bushy tail
Roz's beautiful wedding dress
the potato's long-lasting culinary appeal
potatoes for sale here
the last century's most significant contributions to industry
all vegetables drastically reduced
its universal appeal.

DEVELOPING YOUR OWN STYLE

STYLE

There is, of course, more to good English than a knowledge of correct grammar and correct usage. **Style** is also an important issue.

Style with regard to language, as is the case with style with regard to other things such as dress, refers to a characteristic, personal way of doing things. Most famous writers have a distinctive way of writing. We cannot all become famous writers but we can all improve, to some extent, our personal writing style.

In much of what we write in our day-to-day lives clarity and comprehensibility are extremely important and good grammar has a big role to play in this. However, they are not the only things to be considered if you want to improve your English writing.

For example, if all you want to do is to get your message across then you can write or speak in simple sentences with very simple words. (In grammatical terms a simple sentence is a sentence which consists of one main clause [*see* page 53]). However, this approach can become very monotonous and boring.

In this section we consider some of the ways you can make what you are writing or saying more interesting and more stylish, from the length and structure of your sentences to the vocabulary you choose to use.

Sentence style

Sentence length

One of the easiest ways of introducing variety in your writing is to vary the length of your sentences. A piece of writing that contains sentences of varying length is more likely to capture and retain your reader's attention. From your own point of view as the writer, it is much more interesting and enjoyable to write a piece of prose that contains a variety of lengths of sentence.

The occasional long sentence is quite permissible, provided that it remains clear and unambiguous. You should avoid using too many of these, and you should avoid altogether long sentences which are unnecessarily complicated. These are inclined to confuse readers, or even to make them stop reading the writing in question altogether, because they cannot easily follow what is being said. Thus, sentences like the following should be avoided and should be broken up into shorter ones:

As it was a long trip from our house to my parents' farm, where we were going to celebrate my father's sixtieth birthday, which is on June 20, we decided to break our journey halfway at a hotel which had been recommended by my Aunt Mary, who regularly makes the same journey, and whose judgement we trust because she is an experienced traveller, who is usually quite critical of hotels and restaurants that she encounters when she is travelling.

It has been pointed out above that a piece of writing composed entirely of very short simple sentences can be monotonous and boring. This is the case in the following piece of prose:

I sat my English exam today. It was very difficult. I did badly. I think I will fail. I am dreading getting the results. My parents are going to be very angry. They told me to study harder. I did not. I played football instead. I got into the school team. My parents do not care about that. They want me to go to university. They both did. I do not really want to go. I do not like studying. I am not clever.

However, the occasional very short sentence in a piece of writing with longer sentences can be very effective, as in the passage below. They signify to the reader that something important has happened, thus making the reader pay more attention, and they can make a situation sound more dramatic and so more interesting. The two short sentences in the passage are in bold type.

It was a beautiful day when we started out on our walk. Since there was not a cloud in the sky, and the sun was shining very brightly, we were all wearing light summer clothes. As we had decided to take a picnic, we started, around lunch time, to look for a picturesque spot from which we could admire the view as we ate. Having found the ideal spot, we unpacked all the food and made ourselves comfortable on a blanket, looking forward to basking in the sun. **How wrong we were!** *A few clouds had* *gathered when we were concentrating on finding the right spot and the sky had darkened. Now the heavens opened and the rain poured down. **We got soaked**.*

The middle way

Most sentences in a piece of prose are likely to lie somewhere between the very long and the very short. They are likely to consist of several **clauses**. Extensive information on the various kinds of **clause** is given earlier in the book (*see* pages 53–67).

Sentence structure

You can also introduce variety into your writing and formal speech by varying the number of **clauses** in your sentences, by varying the **types** of clause which you use, and by varying the **position** of clauses in your sentences. In order to achieve such variation you should make yourself familiar with the information on **clauses** and **sentences** given earlier in the grammar section of the book. Then experiment with this information to achieve variety in your writing and formal speech.

Compound sentences

Writing or speaking only in **compound sentences** connected by **coordinating conjunctions** (*see* pages 42 and 217) can be just as monotonous as simple sentences.

If you are aiming for variety and a degree of stylishness avoid a piece of prose like the following:

My daughters are twins and they usually like the same things. They wear the same clothes and they have the same hair styles. They both like music, but Sue likes to sing and Jane likes to dance. They are both learning to play musical instruments, but Jane plays the piano and Sue plays the violin. They both play in the school orchestra and they will both be playing in the end-of-term concert. It takes place next month and most of the members of our family will be there, but my parents will be overseas and so will be unable to attend . . .

Complex sentences

Introduce some **complex sentences** with **subordinating conjunctions** (*see* pages 43 and 218) to create some variety in your work. There is a wide range of conjunctions for you to choose from and a wide range of information given as guidance in the relevant section of this book.

Thus, instead of writing

It was raining and we played indoors.

you can write

Because it was raining we played indoors.

or

Since it was raining we played indoors.

Instead of writing

She worked hard but she failed the exam.

you can write

Although she worked hard, she failed the exam

or

Even though she worked hard she failed the exam.

Instead of writing

I met him at Jane's party and disliked him instantly.

you can write

When I met him at a party I disliked him instantly.

or

As soon as I met him at Jane's party I disliked him.

Alternatively, you can use a **participial phrase** (*see* page 71) instead of a clause.

Thus, you can write

Having arrived at our hotel, we unpacked and went for a walk

instead of

When we arrived at our hotel we unpacked and went for a walk.

Vocabulary

Your choice of **vocabulary** can also greatly influence your style of writing and speaking.

Vocabulary refers to the stock of words that a language is made up of. The English language is made up of a huge number of words, although most educated native speakers of English are likely to have in their own personal stock of words only a fraction of this number. Furthermore, they are likely to use a relatively small number of this personal stock of words in their day-to-day communication.

Active and passive vocabulary

The words that a person is likely to use confidently and regularly are known collectively as that person's **active vocabulary**. The opposite of this is **passive vocabulary**. This consists of the words whose meanings a person knows, although they would not usually use them in the course of their ordinary conversation and writing.

People who are keen to improve their English should try to improve the range of their vocabulary. They may need relatively few words to make themselves understood, but, although comprehensibility is extremely important in speaking and writing, it is not the only issue. If you wish to make your speech or writing more interesting and more stylish you need to introduce a degree of variation into your vocabulary and so improve your word power.

Increasing your word power

How is this to be achieved? There is very little point in simply learning lists of words, perhaps from a dictionary, because things learned in this way tend not to stick in the memory very well. Also, you need to see words in actual use in order to know how you yourself should use them.

Reading can extend your vocabulary quite considerably and this should not be confined to the works of the acknowledged great writers in English. There is a wide range of reading matter available and you should take full advantage of this. Newspapers, for example, can be a useful source of words as well as news. A word of warning, however. Try not to be too much influenced by the level of slang that you may find in some articles in some of the tabloids.

Listening to English radio programmes can also be useful, especially those that concentrate more on talk than music. Television, too, especially 'serious' programmes such as documentaries and those that are concerned with news, current affairs, politics, the arts etc, can also be a useful contributor to your vocabulary stock. Even just talking to and listening to people can be extremely valuable in your attempt to increase your vocabulary.

Dictionaries and thesauruses

To some extent, some language reference books can help improve your word power. In general a thesaurus is more helpful than a dictionary in this respect. A dictionary is a valuable tool when you want to know the meaning of a word, or how to pronounce it, or when you want to find out the origin of a word.

Some of them also supply notes which provide useful advice on usage. Even more useful guidance on usage is provided by those dictionaries which provide example sentences and phrases showing the defined words in action. The dictionaries most likely to provide such example sentences and phrases are those designed for use by learners of English as a foreign or second language.

You are likely to find a thesaurus more helpful than a dictionary in your attempt to increase the extent of your vocabulary. In English, there are two kinds of thesaurus. One type is arranged according to **theme** and the other is, more or less, a dictionary of **synonyms**.

The first thesaurus, published in Britain in 1852, is known as *Roget's Thesaurus*, after its compiler, Peter Mark Roget. It is arranged according to theme. For example, all the words, whatever their part of speech, and all the phrases relating to *fear* are included in the same section and are followed by the words and phrases relating to the opposite of fear, *courage*. Thus we find such nouns as *fright*, *terror* and *panic* and *alarmist*, *scaremonger* and *terrorist* together with adjectives such as *afraid*, *frightened*, *panic-stricken* and verbs such as *take fright*, *be petrified*, *alarm*, *intimidate* in the same section. There, too, are phrases such as *make one's blood run cold* and *make one's hair stand on end*.

Roget's Thesaurus is an extremely valuable reference book but it is a very sophisticated one and it can be quite difficult to use until you become familiar with it. There are other thesauruses, also arranged according to theme in the manner of *Roget's Thesaurus*, but slightly easier to use. Like Roget, they tend to be most useful when you want to write about a particular topic and are seeking the range of vocabulary associated with that topic.

If you want, for example, to avoid repeating a particular word, although you want a word with the same meaning, you will probably find it easier to use the kind of thesaurus which is, in effect, a dictionary of synonyms. (The word *synonym* means a word that has more or less the same meaning as a particular word.)

If, for example, you want to avoid using an overused adjective, such as *nice* or *good*, a synonym-style thesaurus will provide you with a selection of appropriate alternatives. The more helpful of these will have numbered the various meanings of a particular word *and* will have provided example sentences or phrases.

Thus, instead of writing:

*It was a **nice** day yesterday and we decided to go for a drive in the country. We drove through some **nice** scenery and stopped for a really **nice** meal in a restaurant which was run by two very **nice** people. It's a long time since I had such a **nice** day out.*

With the help of a thesaurus you could avoid overusing *nice* and write, for example:

*It was a **sunny** day yesterday and we decided to go for a drive in the country. We drove through some **attractive** scenery and stopped for a really **delicious** meal in a restaurant which was run by two very **agreeable** people. It's a long time since I had such an **enjoyable** day out.*

Likewise, instead of writing:

*My **good** friend Jim is planning to visit us at the end of this month. It is a **good** time for him to come and see us as I am going to be on holiday from work for a **good** two weeks during his visit and we usually have **good** weather at this time of year. It is not the usual holiday season, but I have a **good** reason for taking a break as I have been working a great deal of overtime. I am quite glad that the children are not going to be on holiday because, although they are usually very **good**, they probably would not sit quietly to listen to Jim's stories. He is **a good** conversationalist and has led an interesting life. A very **good** engineer, he has had several very **good** jobs in many parts of the world and loves to talk about his experiences. I cannot wait for him to get here and tell me about them.*

With the help of a thesaurus you could avoid overusing *good* and write, for example:

*My **close** friend Jim is planning to visit us at the end of this month. It is a **convenient** time for him to come and see us as I am going to be on holiday from work for a **full** two weeks during his visit and we usually have **fine*** *weather at this time of year. It is not the usual holiday season but I have a **valid** reason for taking a break as I have been working a great deal of overtime. I am quite glad that the children are not going to be on holiday because, although they are usually very **well-behaved**, they probably would not sit quietly to listen to Jim's stories. He is an **excellent** conversationalist and has led an interesting life. A very **competent** engineer, he has had several very **interesting** jobs in many parts of the world and loves to talk about his experiences. I cannot wait for him to get here and tell me about them.*

These are very simple examples, but they illustrate how you can introduce variation into your vocabulary, perhaps with a little help from a reference book.

Register

When deciding on the vocabulary for your piece of writing or speech you must be careful that you do not use very informal words in a piece of very formal writing or speech, such as a company report. Conversely, you must be careful not to use very formal words in a piece of very informal writing or speech.

The aspect of language that refers to formality and informality is called **register**. It refers to language of a type that is used in a particular social situation. Formal language should be used in formal social situations and informal language in informal situations. Many dictionaries, particularly those specially designed for use by learners of English as a foreign or second language, will often indicate which words are formal and which are informal.

Language formality can be seen as a kind of scale. It starts with the very formal language of formal invitations and legal documents and ends with the slang of much of today's speech. Much of today's written language comes in the middle of the scale. It is neither very formal nor very informal.

People producing written material have much more time than people who are producing instantaneous spoken material in which to choose the exact word they are looking for. Of course, they also have the opportunity to consult thesauruses and dictionaries. This has the result that written English often contains much more innovative and formal vocabulary than the spoken version, unless, of course, the spoken English takes the form of a prepared speech which is to be read aloud.

Keep it simple

There is a danger in having a great deal of time in which to prepare a piece of writing or a speech. You can be faced with the temptation to try to impress people by selecting very difficult words, rather than using those words that come naturally. Although it is a good idea to introduce some variety into your vocabulary, you should resist the temptation to seek out very difficult or pompous-sounding words. This will simply bore your readers or listeners. You will not keep their attention if you are using a great many unnecessarily difficult words which they do not understand.

You should also avoid using a large number of words where a few would be perfectly adequate. If you are too wordy or verbose you are, again, likely to bore, or even confuse, your readers or listeners. Again, you are unlikely to hold their attention.

Adding variety

You can add variety to the vocabulary of writing and so improve your personal style by the careful use of figures of speech such as similes. A **figure of speech** is is a word or phrase that departs from everyday literal language for the sake of comparison, emphasis, clarity or freshness.

A **simile** is a figure of speech in which a thing or person is, for the sake of comparison, said to be *like* another and most include the words *like* or *as*. Examples of similes include:

as calm as a millpond
as cool as a cucumber
as helpless as a babe in arms
as keen as mustard
as neat as a new pin
as poor as a church mouse
as silent as the grave

Another figure of speech found in English writing

is the **metaphor**. Like a simile it uses comparison to create a striking image that can enliven your writing but it does not use the words *like* or *as* that help to identify similes. *I had butterflies in my tummy* is a good example of a metaphor. The words do not mean that the person literally has butterflies in their tummy but the image the words present beautifully illustrates that feeling of nervousness that many of us often experience.

Sometimes correct English writing lacks the fluent use of an English **idiom** which can be used inventively to increase the effect of what is being said. An idiom is a common word or phrase with a culturally understood meaning that differs from what its composite words would suggest. In other words it is a phrase whose meaning cannot easily be understood just from the meanings of the individual words that make up the phrase. Knowing what all the individual words mean in an idiom will not necessarily help you to work out what the idiom is about.

Take, for example, the common English idiom *let the cat out of the bag*. Most people new to it will know all the words in this phrase but they will probably not be able to guess that the phrase means to make known to other people, often accidentally or inappropriately, something that is intended to be kept secret or confidential. If you *swallow something hook, line and sinker*, it does not mean that you are literally copying the actions of a fish in the process of being caught. Instead, it means that you believe something completely (and often naïvely).

There are a great many idioms in the English language. They can add colour and interest to your writing but you should not use too many of them or the clarity of your writing may suffer. You should especially use sparingly those idioms which have been used so often that they have become clichés.

Clichés are expressions which have become so over-used that native speakers of English tend to use them without thinking. They are an important part of the English language (especially so in spoken English) and they can add interest and variety to what you want to say in your writing but it is difficult for learners of the language to become familiar with them and learn how to use them well. Like other aspects of language this requires of lot of practice.

There are some words (particularly relevant to spoken English but which you may wish to include in your written English) which can cause some confusion because they are very similar in some way to other words. These are homophones, homonyms and homographs.

A **homophone** is a word that is pronounced in the same way as another but is spelled in a different way and has a different meaning. For example, **aisle** is a noun meaning a passage between rows of seats in a church, theatre, cinema etc, as in *The bride walked down the aisle on her father's arm* while **isle** is a noun meaning an island, often in used in literary or poetic contexts, but occasionally used in place names, as in *the Isle of Skye*.

A **homonym** is a word that has the same spelling and the same pronunciation as another word, but has a different meaning from it. For example, **bill** is a noun meaning a written statement of money owed, as in *You must pay the bill for the conversion work immediately*; a written or printed advertisement, as in *We were asked to deliver handbills advertising the play;* and a bird's beak, as in *The seagull injured its bill*.

A **homograph** is a word that is spelled the same as another word but has a different meaning, and sometimes pronunciation (heteronym). For example, **sow**, pronounced to rhyme with *low*, is a verb meaning to scatter seeds in the earth, as in *In the spring the gardener sowed some flower seeds in the front garden*, while **sow**, pronounced to rhyme with *how*, is a noun meaning a female pig, as in *The sow is in the pigsty with her piglets*.

(*See* pages 378–384 for more examples of homophones, homonyms and homographs.)

EXERCISES 13

Rewrite the following passage using complex sentences with **subordinating conjunctions** or **participial phrases** instead of **coordinating conjunctions**.

A bad start to the day

I didn't hear my alarm go off yesterday and I overslept. I dressed very quickly but was still very much behind schedule. I was very late and I had no time for breakfast, not even a cup of coffee.

I was late leaving the house and I had to run to the bus stop. I got there on time to catch the bus, but I didn't get on it. There was a long queue in front of me waiting for the same bus and it was soon full.

What was I to do? I could wait for the next bus, but I would be late for work. I had been late twice this month already and my boss would not be pleased. In fact, he would be furious.

I was standing there feeling very depressed and I heard a car's horn sounding. I looked up and saw my friend Jack waving at me from his car. He is a very kind person and he offered me a lift. I would not be late after all!

I arrived at work on time and was able to relax for the first time that morning. Better still, I could have a cup of coffee. I must remember to go out at lunch time and buy a new alarm clock.

ANSWERS 13

The passage below is just for guidance. There are other ways of rewriting the passage.

A bad start to the day

Yesterday I overslept because I didn't hear my alarm going off. Even though I dressed very quickly I was still very much behind schedule. Being very late, I had no time for breakfast, not even a cup of coffee.

I had to run to the bus stop because I was so late leaving the house. Although I got there on time to catch the bus I didn't get on it. As there was a long queue in front of me waiting for the same bus, it was soon full.

What was I to do? I would be late for work if I waited for the next bus. My boss would not be pleased since I had been late twice this month already. In fact, he would be furious.

I suddenly heard a car's horn sounding while I was standing there feeling very depressed. When I looked up I saw my friend Jack waving from his car. Being a very kind person, he offered me a lift to work. I would not be late after all!

Having arrived at work on time, I was able to relax for the first time that morning. Better, still, I could have a cup of coffee. I must remember to go out at lunch time so that I can buy a new alarm clock.

EXERCISES 14

Replace the word **hard** in each of the sentences below. Choose a suitable word for each sentence from the list below.

arduous, difficult, complicated, firm, harsh, industrious, unkind, violent

1 *It had not rained for a long time and the ground was very ………..*
2 *They were all ……….. workers and deserved a pay increase.*
3 *He received a ……….. blow to the head and passed out.*
4 *Whether to go or stay was a ……….. decision for him to make.*
5 *This jigsaw is too ……….. for a child.*
6 *After an ……….. climb up the mountain the climbers were exhausted.*
7 *An exchange of ……….. words between the two sisters led to a bitter family feud.*
8 *Poor farmers lived in very……….. conditions in those days, especially in winter.*

ANSWERS 14

1 *It had not rained for a long time and the ground was very* **firm**.
2 *They were all* **industrious** *workers and deserved a pay increase.*
3 *He received a* **violent** *blow to the head and passed out.*
4 *Whether to go or stay was a* **difficult** *decision for him to make.*
5 *This jigsaw is too* **complicated** *for a child.*
6 *After an* **arduous** *climb up the mountain the climbers were exhausted.*
7 *An exchange of* **unkind** *words between the two sisters led to a bitter family feud.*
8 *Poor farmers lived in very* **harsh** *conditions in those days, especially in winter.*

Words That May Confuse

IDIOMS, CLICHÉS AND EVERYDAY PHRASES

In this last section of the book, there are lists of common English idioms, clichés and everyday phrases, and a few examples of homophones, homonyms and homographs, all of which can cause some confusion to learners of English. To help you become more confident when it comes to including them in your written and spoken English, we have provided example sentences showing them in use.

Common idioms

The list that follows gives a selection of **common idioms** with an explanation of the meaning, the origin of the idiom where appropriate and a short piece of dialogue showing how the idiom is used.

Achilles' heel
This idiom indicates that someone has a weak spot of some kind. (In Greek legend, Achilles is said to have been dipped by his mother in the River Styx in order to make him invulnerable, but his heel was left vulnerable because she was holding him by it and he was killed by an arrow shot through his heel.)
Bill: I'm surprised you decided to fire Lucy.
Tony: I was sorry to have to do it but we had to lose some members of staff and we wanted to keep our best people.
Bill: I thought Lucy was one of those.
Tony: She's very talented but her lack of concentration is her **Achilles' heel**.

acid test

This idiom refers to a test that will prove or disprove something so that there is no doubt. (Nitric acid was once used as a test for gold. If the metal tested was not gold, it decomposed because of the action of the acid on it.)

Sally: Doesn't the new range of cosmetics look wonderful? The packaging is very stylish, isn't it?

Mary: It is and many people have admired it, but **the acid test** will be how well it sells.

have an axe to grind

This idiom means to have a personal or selfish reason to be involved in something. (From a story told by the American politician Benjamin Franklin about an incident in his boyhood when a man asked him to show him how well his grandfather's grindstone worked. The man gave Franklin his own axe to demonstrate on and so got it sharpened for nothing.)

Liz: Jenny must be very fond of her parents-in-law. She's trying to persuade them to buy a house in the street where she and Bob live.

Pat: I don't think that's because she likes them. She has **an axe to grind**.

Liz: What do you mean?

Pat: She's finding it difficult to get a reliable childminder and she thinks it would be hard for them to refuse to look after their grandchildren if they lived close by.

the back of beyond

This idiom refers to a remote place which is difficult to get to and probably has very few people living there.

Sam: You've obviously lived in the city a long time. Were you brought up here?

Ken: No, I came to university here and stayed on. I was brought up on a farm in the north of the country in **the back of beyond**.

beat about the bush

This idiom means to approach a subject in an indirect way, rather than getting straight to the point. (When hunters are shooting game birds people are employed to beat the bushes, heather, etc to make the birds fly up.)

Jane: The new assistant I hired is no good. I'm going to have to let her go, but she's so keen and she really needs the money. I don't know how to tell her.

Sue: There's no point in **beating about the bush**. You're just going to have to tell her straight.

having a bee in your bonnet

This idiom means that you are unable to stop thinking or talking about something so that it becomes an obsession. (A bee trapped under a hat cannot escape and goes buzzing around under it.)

Pat: What's wrong? You look very annoyed.

Kate: I'm annoyed with Ben. He's just spent half-an-hour criticizing me for buying a car.

Pat: I can't say I'm surprised. He **has a bee in his bonnet** about private cars. He thinks everyone should use public transport and save the environment.

Kate: I can sympathize with that, but he has no right to be so nasty to me.

a big fish in a small pond

An important or influential person whose importance is restricted to a small group, organization, area, etc.

Jim: Do you think Pete's wise to take the new job he's been offered?

Ben: No, I don't. It's a very senior job and I'm not sure Pete could cope with it.

Jim: But he has a very senior job in his present company.

Ben: But it's a small firm and Pete's **a big fish in a small pond**. The firm that's offered him the job is a huge multi-national.

burn your bridges/boats
This idiom means to take an action that means that you cannot return to your original position or situation. (If you literally burn your bridges/boat after arriving, you have no means of getting back to where you came from.)
Sam : Did Ben really shout at the boss?
John : Yes, he did and he was very rude to him. I was there when it happened.
Sam: Do you think the boss will forgive him?
John: Absolutely not. Ben's really **burnt his bridges**. The boss fired him and won't give him a reference.

the buck stops here
This idiom is used to indicate the person who is finally responsible for something that has to be dealt with. (The expression refers to a card game such as poker, the buck being a marker passed around to indicate who the dealer is. Harry S. Truman, US President [1945–53], had a sign on his desk with this inscription.)
Will: Why are you going to resign? The mistake wasn't your fault.
Mike: I know it wasn't, but it was the fault of someone in my department and I'm in charge. So I'm afraid it's a case of **the buck stops here**.

carry the can
This idiom means to take the blame or responsibility for something that has gone wrong, even although someone else may be at least partly responsible.
Eve: I can't believe that Joe's been found guilty of cheating in the exam.
Anne: Neither can I, but some people say that he just **carried the can** and that a lot of people were involved in a cheating scam. They got away with it, but Joe didn't.

catch someone red-handed
This idiom means to find someone in the actual act of doing something wrong. (This is reference to the blood on the hands of someone who has just murdered someone.)
Alison: Do you think young Joe really broke into the Brown's house? He seems such a nice quiet boy.
Jenny: There's no doubt about it, I'm afraid. The police **caught him red-handed** when he was trying to sell some of the stolen jewellery.

catch someone with their hand in the till
This idiom, means to discover someone in the act of stealing or doing something dishonest.
Paul: I hear the company accountant's been fired.
Robbie: Yes. They say he's been **caught with his hand in the till**. The auditors have found out that he's been embezzling money for months.

chalk and cheese
This idiom is used to emphasize a measure of how completely different two things are.
Mary: Amy and Lily are sisters, but they're as different as **chalk and cheese**.
Kate: I agree. They don't look the least alike and they have completely different personalities.

cross that bridge when you come to it
This idiom means to worry about a problem or try to cope with it only when it actually affects you.
Mary: It's a lovely flat and we can just about afford the rent between us, but what if the landlord puts the rent up?
Alice: We'll **cross that bridge when we come to it**. Let's go and tell the landlord we'll take it before someone else takes it.

be at daggers drawn
This idiom means that two people are being extremely hostile towards each other. (This is a reference to people pulling out their daggers when they were ready to fight.)

Amy: I didn't know that Dave was Tom's brother. They never seem to speak each other.

Pam: They don't. They've been **at daggers drawn** since their father died more than ten years ago.

Amy: What did they quarrel about?

Pam: I've no idea, but it was something to do with the money left to them by their father.

a rough diamond

This idiom refers to a person who behaves in rather a rough manner but who has some very good qualities.

Ken: What do you think of Sue's new boyfriend?

Alice: The first time I met him he seemed a bit boorish, but he's **a rough diamond**. He's really very kind and helpful.

Ken: I much prefer him to her previous boyfriend. He was very smooth and polite on the surface, but he had a really nasty side to him.

dog eat dog

This idiom is used to refer to a situation in which rivals or opponents are prepared to do anything at all to get what they want.

Dave: My son's just graduated and he's job-hunting.

Bob: Unemployment's so high just now. It's not a good time to be looking for a job.

Dave: No, it's not. There's a lot of competition. It's a case of **dog eat dog** out there.

get (all) your ducks in a row

This idiom means to get everything organized and under control.

Liz: Jill always looks exhausted. She's really not coping with her job and the children.

Mary: She's in a difficult situation, but she really needs to **get her ducks in a row**. She can't do her job properly until she gets help with childcare.

Dutch courage
This idiom refers to a confidence or lack of nervousness that has been brought about by consuming alcohol. (This is perhaps a reference to a former Dutch custom of drinking alcohol before going into battle.)
Pete: It's a bit early for you to be drinking.
Mark: I need a bit of **Dutch courage**. I'm going on a date with Sally and I'm really nervous.
Pete: I'm sure you'll be fine. Don't drink too much!

be at the end of your tether
This idiom means that you are no longer able to tolerate or put up with something. (A tether is literally a rope that is used to tie up an animal, such as a goat, and that extends a certain distance to let the animal graze.)
Janet: You look very tired, Molly.
Molly: I'm exhausted and **at the end of my tether**.
Janet: Why's that?
Molly: I'm hardly getting any sleep because of my upstairs neighbours. They're students and they play loud music all night.

flog a dead horse
This idiom means to go on trying to rouse interest or enthusiasm in something when this is no longer of interest, making your efforts likely to be unsuccessful.
Diane: Jack keeps trying to get Jenny to forgive him for cheating on her, but he's **flogging a dead horse**.
Lily: He certainly is. Jenny has no intention of forgiving him. Her last boyfriend cheated on her and she won't put up with that sort of treatment again.

with flying colours
With great success. (This is a reference to a ship leaving a place of battle with its colours or flag still flying, rather than being lowered in surrender.)

Frank: My son's just got his exam results. He's passed **with flying colours**!

Ben: That's great, especially as he was nervous about his results.

Frank. He was and I can see he's very relieved!

go by the board

This idiom is used to indicate that something is being abandoned or is no longer likely to be possible or successful. (This is a nautical reference. The expression originally meant literally to go overboard and vanish.)

Jill: Are you still thinking of going back to work full-time after the summer?

Wendy: No, my work plans have **gone by the board**. I'm having another baby.

Jill: That's great news! Congratulations!

have green fingers

This idiom means to be very skilful at growing plants.

Kate: I'm looking after my mother's house plants and I'm scared they're going to die. My mother has **green fingers**, but I'm hopeless with plants.

Helen: Remember to water them, but don't water them too much. They should be OK.

hit the ground running

This idiom means to begin some kind of new activity immediately and energetically. (A reference to soldiers running swiftly into battle immediately after leaving a helicopter or being dropped by parachute.)

Lucy: I must say our spring fashion range looks very good.

Emma: It does, but there's a lot of competition around. We really need to find some exciting ways to promote our range and **hit the ground running** when we launch it.

hit the sack/hit the hay

This idiom means to go to bed.

John: Mark and I are going clubbing later. Want to come?
Dan: I can't. I've a busy day tomorrow. I'm going to **hit the sack**.

the jewel in the crown
This idiom refers to the most valuable or successful thing associated with someone or something.
Susan: What a wonderful painting.
Jennifer: Yes, it is, isn't it? The gallery has a marvellous collection, but this is definitely **the jewel in the crown**.

jump on the bandwagon
This idiom means to become involved in something because it is fashionable or because it will be profitable, although you may not be really interested in it. (From the brightly coloured vehicle carrying a band at the head of a procession which often encourages people to follow the procession.)
Tom: I hear George has gone into the real estate business. I didn't know he was interested in property.
David: George's not the least bit interested in it. The property market's doing very well just now and he's just **jumping on the bandwagon**.

kill two birds with one stone
This idiom means to carry out two aims by means of one action.
Sue: What are you planning to do in the city?
Rosemary: I'm going to **kill two birds with one stone**. I have an appointment with my dentist and I need to collect some books I ordered from the central library.

be left holding the baby
This idiom means to be left to cope with a situation on your own which was really the responsibility of other people.
Joe: What's wrong with you? You look really cross.
Mark: I'm furious. My boss is responsible for organizing the sales conference, but he's suddenly decided to go on holiday. I've been left **holding the baby**.

let off steam

This idiom means to do something active that helps you get rid of your excess energy or strong feelings about something. (This is a reference to steam being released from a steam engine in order to reduce pressure.)

Harry: I don't think Dad should write such a rude letter to the store manager.

Bob: Don't worry. He won't send it. He's just **letting off steam**. He was so annoyed when it wouldn't work.

lock, stock and barrel

This idiom is used to emphasize how complete something is, with everything included. (This is a reference to the main parts of a gun.)

Ben : Has Sam really bought a house?

James: Yes, he has. He bought it with the money his aunt left him.

Ben: He'll have to buy furniture now.

James: No, he won't. He bought the contents and house **lock, stock and barrel**.

make a mountain out of a molehill

This idiom means to exaggerate the extent of a difficult situation or problem to make it seem much worse than it really is.

Lucy: What did Tony say to Jane? She says that she'll never speak to him again.

Jill: Emma was there when it happened and she said that Tony was just teasing Jane. He apologized when he saw she was upset, but she wouldn't listen.

Lucy: I'm sure Emma's right. Jane's always **making mountains out of molehills**.

the moment of truth

This idiom refers to a crucial time when you find out whether something has proved to be successful, will work etc. (This is a translation of the Spanish expression *el momento de la verdad*, which refers to the moment in a bullfight when the matador is about to kill the bull.)

Mary: Your brother's spent ages working on that old car.

Pat: He certainly has and he's spent quite a lot of money on it.

Mary: I hope it's worth all that time and money.

Pat: So do I. He's taking it for a test drive tomorrow. That'll be **the moment of truth**.

the final nail in someone's coffin

This idiom refers to something, often the latest in a series of events, which helps to bring about someone's ruin or destruction.

Bob: Joe's just told me that Mike's been fired.

Bill: Has he? I can't say I'm surprised. Quite a few customers have complained about him recently.

Bob: Apparently the boss heard him being very rude to one of our most regular customers this morning. That was **the final nail in his coffin**. The boss told him to leave immediately.

once in a blue moon

This idiom means almost never or very rarely. (A blue moon is the appearance of the third full moon in a season that has four full moons, instead of the usual three and as a blue moon occurs only every two or three years, the term *blue moon* is used to mean a rare event, as in this phrase *once in a blue moon*.)

Joan: I remember that you and Pete were real movie buffs at college. Do you go to the movies much these days?

Alice: **Once in a blue moon**. It's hard to get out with three young children. We usually have to make do with DVDs.

be over the moon

This idiom means to be extremely happy or joyful.

Lucy: Amy seems in a very good mood today.

Anne: She's **over the moon**. She's just got engaged. She's getting married next year.

paddle your own canoe
This idiom means to be independent enough to manage your own affairs without help or support from anyone else.
Jane: Jenny has finally decided to leave home.
Sue: And about time too! She's far too old to be so dependent on her parents.
Jane: Yes, it really is time for her to **paddle her own canoe**.

paint the town red
This idiom means to go out and celebrate something, usually in a lively, extravagant way.
Anne: I can't come to the meeting tonight. I'm going out.
Mary: What are you doing?
Anne: We're going to **paint the town red**. We're celebrating our daughter's graduation.
Mary: Have a good time!

be par for the course
This idiom refers to what usually happens or what might be expected to happen, often used with reference to something undesirable or bad. (This is a golfing reference to the number of strokes that would be made in a perfect round on a golf course.)
Jack: Dan's had to close down his computer business.
Will: I'm afraid that's **par for the course** for small businesses these days.
Jack: Yes. The recession's hit a lot of them very badly.

pass the buck
This idiom means to try to shift the blame or responsibility for something onto someone else instead of accepting it yourself. (The expression refers to a card game such as poker, the buck being a marker passed around to indicate who the dealer is.)
Pete: The sales are very bad again this month. It's all the fault of the new sales manager. He's hopeless.
Ken: You're quite right, but he's trying to **pass the buck**. He says the poor sales are down to the marketing department.

pie in the sky

This idiom refers to an idea, hope or plan, relating to something good, that is unlikely to happen. (This phrase is from the words of a song by Joe Hill, an American who wrote many radical songs for a labour organisation known as the Industrial Workers of the World: 'You'll get pie in the sky when you die.')

Sally: Joe was desperate to be a doctor when we were at school but it was all **pie in the sky**. Although he worked really hard, he was not at all academic.

Amy: It was a real shame, but I believe he went into his father's business and is doing very well.

the rat race

This idiom refers to a way of life in which people compete aggressively for success in business etc.

Mark: I'm amazed that Steve's given up his job and gone to live in the country. He was doing so well.

Goerge: Yes. He was making a lot of money as a stockbroker, but he got really tired of the financial world and he was doing nothing but work. He hardly ever saw his wife and children. He's tired of **the rat race**.

Mark: I think he'll be back. Country life'll be too quiet for him.

a red herring

This idiom refers to a piece of information, sometimes a false clue laid deliberately, which misleads someone. (A reference to a strong-smelling fish whose scent could mislead hunting dogs and distract them from their prey.)

Molly: Do the police think that Frank was killed by a burglar?

Sue: Not any more. They did at first because his apartment was in such a mess. Now they think that was done by the murderer as **a red herring**. They think that someone went to Frank's place intending to kill him, not to steal anything.

rest on your laurels

This idiom refers to the fact that you are not trying very hard for further success because you are relying on the good reputation brought about by past successes. (This is a reference to the ancient Greek practice of crowning successful poets and winners with laurel wreaths.)

Jim: Bob didn't play very well in the match today. If he doesn't start trying harder he'll get dropped from the team.

Frank: I'm sure you're right. He used to be the best player by far but there are now quite a few good young players in the team. Bob really can't afford to **rest on his laurels**.

score an own goal

This idiom means to do something that is harmful or disadvantageous to your own interests. (This is a reference to kicking a ball into your own team's goal.)

Mike: Did Kate get the job?

Sam: No, she didn't and she **scored an own goal** at her interview. She told the owner of the firm that one of the other applicants had been in prison.

Mike: What happened?

Sam: They gave the job to the woman who had been in prison. Apparently the boss had been in prison himself when he was young and sympathized with ex-prisoners.

shoot yourself in the foot

This idiom means to do something which is disadvantageous or harmful to yourself or to your situation.

John: I'm not taking my car back to that garage again. The guy charged me a fortune for servicing it.

Tom: I've stopped using them. They kept putting their prices up.

John: They're **shooting themselves in the foot**. Everyone's going to go somewhere cheaper.

sing from the same hymn sheet

This idiom means to show agreement with each other about something, especially in public.

Chief executive: There may be minor differences of opinion among members of the board, but it is vital that we all **sing from the same hymn sheet** at the annual general meeting.

Company accountant: I quite agree. We must make sure that shareholders continue to have confidence in the company.

smell a rat

This idiom means to suspect that something is not right or normal. (This is a reference to a dog hunting rats by scent.)

Sally: How did Alice find out that her husband was having an affair?

Lily: She **smelt a rat** when he started saying he had to work late every night. Then a friend told her that she had seen him a couple of times in a club with his secretary.

Sally: What happened then?

Lily: He admitted to the affair and moved out.

stab someone in the back

This idiom means to behave treacherously towards someone, often a friend or colleague, or to betray someone.

Ben: I thought Pete was my friend, but he **stabbed me in the back**. I told him in complete confidence that I had pretended to be off ill for a few days when I had really taken my kids on holiday.

Harry: So what?

Ben: Pete went and told our boss. It turns out that he wants my job. He was trying to get me sacked.

Harry: But you still have your job, don't you?

Ben: Only just. I got an official warning.

stick to your guns

This idiom means to refuse to change your decision or opinion about something, no matter what happens. (This is reference to a soldier who keeps firing at the enemy even when his life is in great danger.)

Liz: Is Pat still thinking of reporting her boss for bullying her?
Jane: I think so, but some of her colleagues are trying to persuade her not to. They say that management will be on the side of the boss and will take no notice of her complaint.
Liz: I hope she **sticks to her guns**. Her boss has been horrible to her. He deserves to be punished.

a storm in a teacup
This idiom means a great fuss over something not at all important. The American version of this idiom is a 'tempest in a teacup'.
Lucy: Was Alice hurt? Somebody said she'd been bitten by a dog.
Jenny: No. The whole thing was **a storm in a teacup**. The dog just jumped up on her but it was a large dog and Alice caused a big fuss about it.
Lucy: Well, she is terrified of dogs, so you can't blame her.

take the biscuit
This idiom refers to something that is particularly surprising, shocking, or annoying.
Bob: My brother's always borrowing my things without asking me, but this **takes the biscuit**. He's gone away for a few days and borrowed my car and I need it to get to work.
Mark: How do you know?
Bob: He's left me a note!

a tempest in a teacup *see* a storm in a teacup

throw someone a curve/curved ball
This idiom, more common in American English, means to surprise someone by doing something unexpected and perhaps putting them at some kind of disadvantage. (The expression has its origins in baseball when a curved ball suddenly and unexpectedly swerves away from the person trying to hit the ball just as it reaches his or her bat.)

Mike: John and Will were expecting their grandfather to leave them a lot of money. They were planning to use it to set up their own business.

Jack: What happened?

Mike: The old man **threw them a curve** and changed his will just before he died. He had lung cancer and he left all his money to a cancer charity. John and Will were shocked but there was nothing they could do about it.

throw a spanner in the works

This idiom means to stop, prevent or delay a plan, project, etc from going ahead.

Phil: You're holiday starts next week, right?

Harry: Not any more. My boss has **thrown a spanner in the works**. He wants me to go on a management course then.

Phil: That's too bad.

tighten your belt

This idiom means to reduce the amount of money which you spend regularly. (If you spend less money on food and so lose weight you will have to tighten your belt to hold up your jeans.)

Jackie: Prices seem to keep going up and up.

Lorna: But our pay's not going up. With three children we're finding it difficult to manage.

Jackie: So are we. We're really having to **tighten our belts**.

too big for your boots

This idiom means that you have become very conceited and think that you are superior to others.

Julie: Are you still friendly with Amy?

Sarah: No, not any longer. She's become far **too big for her boots** since she married Mike Brown. He's very rich.

turn over a new leaf

This idiom means to start to act in a better, more acceptable way.

Teacher: We're very pleased with Paul's work this term. It shows a great improvement and he's certainly working much harder.

Paul's mother: Yes, thank goodness. He's spending a lot more time studying. He really seems to have **turned over a new leaf**.

twist someone's arm

This idiom means to try to persuade or force someone to do something that they really do not want to do. (If you literally twist someone's arm you use physical force.)

Peter: I thought you weren't coming to Jill's party, Joe. You've always said you hate parties.

Joe: I do hate them. I told Jill several times that I wasn't coming, but **she twisted my arm**. You know how determined she is!

be up in the air

This idiom means to be still undecided or uncertain about something.

Jill: Where are you and Jim going on holiday this year?

Trisha: Our plans are still **up in the air**. We'd like to go to Greece with my brother and sister-in-law but it's very difficult for us all to get off work at the same time.

Jill: I hope you can sort something out.

Trisha: So do I. We'll have to book soon if we're going to get a reasonably priced flight.

be up in arms

This idiom means to protest in a very angry way. ('Arms' in this sense means 'weapons'.)

John: Apparently they're planning to extend the airport. They're thinking of adding another runway. The people who live near the airport are **up in arms**. They are planning to hold a protest.

Mary: I'm not surprised. The noise from the planes is terrible at the moment. Goodness knows what it will be like if there are more flights.

wash your hands of someone/something
To indicate that you are no longer going to be responsible for, or involved with, someone or something. (From a reference in the Bible to such an action by Pontius Pilate after the crucifixion of Jesus.)
Wendy: Jill's teaching young Tom to play the piano, isn't she?
Sue: She was, but not any more. She says that Tom has a lot of talent, but he just refuses to practise. She's **washed her hands of him**.

Clichés

Clichés arise from several different areas of English. Sometimes a cliché is just a very common idiom which has become over-used. It is very easy for someone to get into the habit of using an idiom again and again without being aware of this. Such **clichés from idioms** include:

between a rock and a hard place
Faced with two equally unpleasant or unacceptable choices.
John: I'm going to stay with my parents at the end of the week but I can't decide whether to go by train or plane. I'm **between a rock and a hard place**. The plane is quicker but it's very expensive while the train is much slower but it's also much cheaper.
Phil: I suppose it depends which matters most to you—time or money.

fall on your sword
Historically to commit suicide in this way, but the modern cliché means to resign from a position of power or importance, often because you have been found committing some kind of crime or wrongdoing which would have resulted in your being fired anyway.
Bill: Did you hear about Frank's father?
Sam: Yes. He's been arrested for fraud.
Bill: He's a fairly senior politician. Will he be fired from the administration?
Sam: I think he'll **fall on his sword**. Politicians usually do when something like that happens.

flavour of the month
A person or thing that is particularly popular at a particular time, although this is likely to last only for a short time.

Trisha: This toy was **flavour of the month** at Christmas and it was almost impossible to find it. Now none of the kids will play with it.
Rose: I know. They've all moved on to some new toy.

the jury's still out
No decision has yet been reached or an issue has not been resolved.
Harry: Has your family decided where to go on holiday yet?
Peter: Every member of the family has a vote and **the jury's still out**. If we can't agree Mum gets to choose.

keep the wolf from the door
To earn enough money for your basic needs, such as food.
Jack: I really need to look for a job that pays more.
Ken: Me too. I need more money just to **keep the wolf from the door**. I certainly can't afford any luxuries.

leave no stone unturned
To try by every means possible to find or do something.
Mary: The police haven't found the child's killer yet. Everyone is so upset by it all.
Jane: I know, but the report in the local paper says that they're **leaving no stone unturned** in their efforts to find whoever is responsible.
Mary: They're certainly asking all the neighbours for information, but they don't seem to have made much progress.

a level playing field
A situation which is completely fair to everyone involved because none of the people taking part has any advantage over the others.
Ben: Some people say that the college gives preference to wealthier students.
Sally: The college authorities have denied that. They say that entrance to the college is **a level playing field**.

a loose cannon
A person who is apt to behave in a unpredictable or reckless fashion and cannot be relied upon not to cause trouble or do something embarrassing.
Jackie: Should we ask Sue to come clubbing with us?
Alice: I don't think so. She can be such **a loose cannon**. Last time she had a bit too much to drink and started shouting at people.
Jackie: I'd forgotten about that. We'll definitely not ask her!

move the goalposts
To change the aims, conditions and rules relating to a project after it is under way.
Roger: Why haven't you started building the extension to your house?
Harry: We haven't got planning permission yet. The officials keep **moving the goalposts**.

open the floodgates
To remove some form of control or restriction so that it makes it possible for a huge number of people to do something.
Ben: The tennis club is getting a bit short of members. I wonder if more people would join if we dropped the minimum age qualification?
Joe: The trouble is that might **open the floodgates**. We don't want a whole lot of very young children joining.
Ben: Well, as a compromise, how about we keep the age limit, but lower it?
Joe: Good idea. Let's raise it at the next committee meeting.

Of course, not all clichés are idioms. Many of them are simply phrases that have become over-used. Some examples of **clichés from over-used phrases** are included in the pages that follow.

an accident waiting to happen
A situation which has always had the potential to be dangerous and which might result in injury or tragedy at any time.
Will: That old burnt-out house is **an accident waiting to happen**. They should pull it down before someone gets hurt.
Sam: They certainly should. The neighbourhood kids are all playing there.

the end of an era
When used correctly the word *era* suggests something relatively important or a considerable length of time. It is used of an important period of history or period of time characterized by a particular feature, event or person, as in *the Victorian era*. As a modern cliché, *the end of an era* is often used to refer to a fairly unimportant event or short-lived period.
June: It's the **end of an era.** Our next-door neighbours are moving house. We've lived next door to each other for six years.
Lucy: You are going to miss them.
June: I certainly will. I'm feeling really depressed about it.

a hidden agenda
A secret or unrevealed motive behind some plan or action.
Jim: I'm surprised that Mark is in favour of the new office block. We're all protesting against it.
Jason: Ah, but Mark has **a hidden agenda**. His father-in-law is the property developer behind the office scheme.
Jim: Well, that explains it.

it goes with the territory
Used of a particular kind of problem or difficulty that often occurs in connection with a particular kind of situation.
Amy: Jim is so much more stressed since he got promoted at work. He used to be such a laid-back person.
Rose: A lot of senior managers suffer from stress. **It goes with the territory**.

it's the thought that counts
A comment or response made on the giving of a gift that has not cost very much. Sometimes the comment is made ironically to refer to a low-cost gift when a higher-priced gift would have been more appropriate.
Jenny: What did your son give you for your birthday?
Meg: He gave me this little book of poems.
Jenny: It certainly is very small.
Meg: But it's by my favourite poet and my son spent ages looking for a copy. Besides, **it's the thought that counts**.

Amy: My brother had obviously forgotten all about my birthday. He arrived late last night with a bunch of flowers that he must have bought from the local petrol station. Still, **it's the thought that counts**!
Diane: You're lucky. I can't remember when my brother last remembered my birthday.

last but not least
Used when giving a list of names or items when there is no particular order of merit.
Jane: I am so pleased to have won the championship. I want to thank my parents, my sister and brother, my cousin Tom and, **last but not least**, my friends Sue and Lucy for their continuing support.

a merciful release
Used to say that you think a person's death was a good thing for that person because it put an end to the suffering caused by a long, painful illness.
Mary: My grandfather died last night.
Alice: I'm sorry to hear that. You must be very sad.
Mary: I am, but actually it was **a merciful release**. He had terminal cancer and was in terrible pain.

needs no introduction
Used by someone who is introducing a person to a group of people. In spite of saying this, they often go on to give an introduction, sometimes a long one.
John: Our last speaker, Sally Brown, **needs no introduction**. She is one of our most talented actresses and many of you will recognize her from her TV appearances. She is particularly well known for her charitable work and has raised lots of money for children's charities in particular.

one hundred and ten per cent
Used to emphasize the great amount of effort used to do something. The maximum mathematical percentage is, in fact, one hundred per cent.
Bill: What qualifications are you looking for in your new assistant?
Jack: I want someone with the right academic qualifications and with business experience but most of all, I want someone who will give **one hundred and ten per cent** to the job. Someone who won't complain about having to work late or come in early.

a race against time
Used to describe an extremely urgent situation.
Mike: The mine has collapsed and some of the miners are trapped underground. It's going to be **a race against time** to get them out alive.
Bob: It's certainly a very dangerous situation.

and the rest is history
Used to indicate that no more need be said about a subject because the details are already well known to the listeners.
Anne: Jack seems to give a great deal of money to local charities. Was he born in this area?
Mary: Yes, he was born of very poor parents in a slum down by the dock. He started work at a very young age doing just about anything. Then he set up his own clothing company **and the rest is history**.

Anne: Well, he's now a millionaire several times over and a very generous man.

these things happen
Used to remind someone who may have experienced some kind of misfortune that bad things happen to people all the time.
Dave: Sam's been laid off. The firm he works for is closing down.
Bill: I'm sorry to hear he's lost his job, but **these things happen**. And we *are* in the middle of a recession.

time will tell
A cliché suggesting that the outcome of something will not be known for quite a long time.
Sally: I hear Joe's still in hospital. Is he going to be all right?
Meg: **Only time will tell**. He suffered some terrible injuries in the accident.
Sally: We'll just have to hope for the best but it is a very worrying situation.

too numerous to mention
Used in more formal spoken contexts supposedly to mean that there are too many people or things involved to mention them all by name. In fact, the phrase is often used as an introduction to a list of the names.
Jack: I would also like to thank the volunteers who helped to make the event such a great success. They are **too numerous to mention**, but many thanks to Sue, Amy, Anne, Diane, Lucy, Pat, Jim, Ben, Joe, John, Mark, and Steve.

the usual suspects
Used to describe the people who are usually involved in something. ('Round up the usual suspects' from *Casablanca*, Warner Bros, 1942.)
Joanna: Were there many people at Sally's barbecue?
Shirley: Not really. It was mostly just **the usual suspects**.

Some of the phrases used as clichés have been in use for a long time and some of them are more formal or even more archaic than you would expect to find in the context in which they are being used. These **archaic** or **more formal clichés** include:

bow to the inevitable
To have to tolerate or accept a situation, however unpleasant, because you cannot avoid it.
Sally: It's dreadful that the landlord's not renewing our lease.
Jane: It is, but he's not going to change his mind. We'll just have to **bow to the inevitable**.
Sally: You're right. We need to look for somewhere else to live.

by the same token
In the same way or for the same, or a similar, reason.
Ben: The students are furious that they're not allowed to leave the school at lunch time anymore.
Joshua: I'm sure they are, but, **by the same token**, the parents are mostly very pleased. It means the kids can't buy junk food at lunch time and they can't get into any trouble.

a daunting prospect
Something very difficult or alarming that you have to face or deal with.
Emma: We love the house and we'd like to buy it, but it needs a lot of work done. We'd have to do it ourselves. That's **a daunting prospect**.
Jessica: It certainly is. Neither of you has ever done any of that kind of work before.

dulcet tones
Sweet or musical tones. This cliché is mostly used ironically.
Rob: We knew we were home when we heard our neighbour's **dulcet tones** shouting at her poor husband.
Pete: I bet you wanted to go away again immediately.

a moot point
Something that is not at all certain but is doubtful or needs to be debated. [A moot court is a method of teaching law and legal skills that requires students to analyze and argue both sides of a hypothetical legal case.]
Lily: We're going for a meal to the Gourmet Scene tonight. We'd better make a reservation. It's still the best restaurant in town.
Rose: That's **a moot point**. There are one or two others that are just as popular now.

pale into insignificance
Used to indicate that something which seems very bad, or unfortunate does not seem quite so bad when compared with something which is much worse.
Jenny: I was feeling very depressed yesterday. I've just lost my job and now I've got to get out of my flat. But my problems **pale into insignificance** compared with Sue's.
Sarah: What's wrong with Sue?
Jenny: She's having tests for breast cancer.

speculation is rife
A cliché popular with journalists indicating that a lot of people are forming opinions about something and spreading these around without knowing the facts of the situation.
Speculation is rife that police have arrested a member of the murder victim's family. Up till now, the police have neither confirmed nor denied that this is the case.

Some clichés add very little meaning to what is being said. They can be described as **fillers**—phrases which fill up space rather than adding significantly to the meaning. Fillers give you thinking time in a conversation and although such clichés can be annoying they help to make a conversation flow along. Without them conversation would be more stilted. Such **filler clichés** include the following:

at the end of the day
Another of today's most irritating and overused clichés, used in much the same way as **when all is said and done** (*see below*) and often used almost meaninglessly.
Kim: My ex can say what he likes but **at the end of the day** it's my decision whether I go out with Tim or not.
Kirsty: I think you are quite right.

at this moment in time
One of today's most overused clichés which really just means now or just now.
Mr Brown: **At this moment in time**, we have no plans to get rid of any staff.
Jim: What about in the future?
Mr Brown: We can't really say. It depends on the company's financial situation over the next few months.

if you ask me
In my opinion.
Joan: **If you ask me**, Harry's thinking of leaving.
Trisha: What makes you think that?
Joan: Well, he's always saying how bored he is and he's been looking at job vacancies in the local paper.

in all honesty
To be frank, to be honest.
Hayley: Shall we go for a drink after work?
Julia: I'm too tired. **In all honesty**, I just want to go home to bed.

in point of fact
A rather meaningless phrase, rather like *in fact*.
Ken: I wouldn't know John if I met him in the street. **In point of fact,** I don't think I know him at all.
Ian: I must introduce you sometime.

mark my words
Pay attention to what I'm going to say.
Lottie: Sally and Tom have just got engaged.
Mary: **Mark my words**. It won't last. Tom's been engaged at least three times before but he's never made it to the altar.
Lottie: You're joking. Why ever not?
Mary: He just can't commit himself. He gets engaged and then he breaks it off.

the thing is
A filler used to pre-empt an explanation that you are about to make.
Amy: I'm not sure whether I'll be able to play tennis with you tomorrow. **The thing is** my parents are away and I have to walk their dog.
Rosemary: Let's leave it till next week, then.

when all is said and done
This phrase is sometimes used to refer to the most important point of a situation, but it is often used almost meaninglessly.
Ken: Hopefully, my son will realize that he needs to spend more time studying if he's to pass the exams. We're doing all we can to encourage him but **when all is said and done** he is the only one that can do anything about it.
Mike: As long as he doesn't leave it too late. The exams are quite soon.

Everyday phrases

There are many expressions used in everyday communication that are an essential part of spoken English and you may wish to use these in any written work involving dialogue. Some of these expressions are interjections (often followed by an exclamation mark) that are used to express emotion or reaction, such as excitement, surprise, annoyance, disgust, joy, pain, etc. Sometimes interjections consist of single words, sometimes they consist of short phrases or very short sentences, and sometimes they consist of just a sound. In many cases interjections provide the links that help conversation to move along smoothly.

A speaker simply cannot be considered fluent without having the ability to use some of these everyday phrases. Yet it can be difficult to acquire information about this feature of English. Dictionaries, especially the smaller ones, do not provide such information and even the larger ones do not necessarily cover this subject in enough detail.

Of course, listening skills come in useful here and you can learn a great deal from listening to English-language radio and television programmes. When doing so it will be helpful to make your own list of everyday phrases, memorize them and then try them out in a conversation. This is an excellent way of increasing your knowledge of the vocabulary of spoken English but some extra help will prove valuable and this is provided in the list that follows.

about time too!
You use this rather rude expression to indicate that someone has arrived late or has taken a long time to do something.
Locksmith: That's all the locks on your doors and windows changed.
Mrs Smith: **About time too!** I didn't think it would take that long.
Locksmith: I worked as fast as I could. There are a lot of windows in this house.

ah!
You use this interjection in various ways. It can be used to express a variety of emotions such as pleasure, surprise or disagreement.
Bill: **Ah!** That was a really delicious meal.
Mary: It certainly was. The new chef has made a huge difference.

ahem!
A sound like a short cough made by someone who is trying to attract attention, sometimes in a difficult or embarrassing situation.
Jill: Let's ask John to organize the meeting. He's not working at the moment and has plenty of free time.
John: **Ahem!** I heard that and it's not true. I'm working freelance and I've got plenty to do.
Jill: Sorry, John! I didn't see you there.

alas
This expression can be used to show that you are sad or sorry about something, but it is sometimes used ironically or humorously.
Bob: I was going to offer to pay half the restaurant bill, but, **alas**, my brother paid it before I had a chance to offer.
Ken: That's fair enough, isn't it? He's a wealthy lawyer and you're still a student.

all right
You use this expression when you wish to say *Yes* to something that someone has asked you.
Sue: I'm going shopping. Do you want to come?
Katie: **All right**. I need a new dress, anyway.

as a matter of fact
You can use this expression in two ways. You can use it to add a piece of interesting or surprising information to what has just been said.
Jack: I don't think this firm can last much longer. I think we should start looking for other jobs.
Will: You're right. **As a matter of fact**, I've already started looking. I've made an appointment with a recruitment agency.

You can also use this expression to indicate that the truth about a situation is the opposite of what has just been stated.
Amy: Was the air fare very expensive?
Jill: No, **as a matter of fact**, it was surprisingly cheap. It cost a lot more last year.

believe it or not
You use this expression when you are mentioning something that is true but very unlikely or surprising.
Matthew: Have you found a flat yet?
Ken: Yes. **Believe it or not**, we've found quite a cheap one in the city centre. The owner's abroad and just wants someone to take care of it.
Matthew: That was lucky.

believe you me
You use this expression in order to stress the truth of what you are going to say or have said.
Jane: **Believe you me**, Joe will regret not going to university.
Mark: I think you're right, but he's really keen on this job he's been offered.

Jane: That's just because it's quite well paid and he wants to get some money fast. It doesn't offer very good promotion prospects.

by all means
You use this expression when you are telling someone that you are happy for them to do something.
Jade: Please can I leave work a bit earlier today? It's my father's sixtieth birthday and we're giving him a surprise party.
Boss: **By all means** take us much time as you need and give your father my best wishes.

by the way
You use this expression when you mention something which is connected in some way with what has just been said.
Jack: I visited Sam yesterday. **By the way**, he's moving to a new flat.
Harry: Can you give me his new address?
Jack: Of course. I've got it right here.

come on!
You say this expression to someone when you want them to hurry or to do something.
Joe: **Come on**, Tom! We'll miss the plane!
Tom: We'll be there in a minute. We've still got plenty of time.
Joe: No we haven't. It's the rush hour!

come to think of it
You use this expression when you have just thought of or remembered something.
Michael: Apparently, Ben's not very well. He's going to the hospital for some tests.
George: I'm sorry to hear that. **Come to think of it**, he's not been going to the gym recently but I just thought he was busy. I didn't know he was ill.

don't bank on it

You use this expression when you want to advise someone not to rely on something happening.

Mary: Sue said that she'd help me look after my sister's baby tomorrow. I was feeling a bit nervous about it.

Emma: **I wouldn't bank on it**. Sue doesn't always keep her promises.

don't say that!

You use this expression when someone says something that you don't want to be true.

Pete: I've had a quick look at your car and I think it might need a new engine.

Bill: **Don't say that!** That'll cost a fortune!

Pete: I could be wrong but you'd better get a mechanic to look at it right away.

dream on!

You use this expression in an informal context to indicate to someone that something is not at all practical or not at all likely to happen.

Tara: I'd love to have a flat overlooking the park.

Mark: **Dream on!** The monthly rent would be more than your annual salary.

for goodness' sake

You use this expression when you are very annoyed or surprised.

Mother: **For goodness' sake**, Lisa, get up and get dressed. We've got guests coming to lunch.

Lisa: OK, I'm just getting up. There's plenty of time.

Mother: No there isn't. I need you to help me tidy the house.

good!

You use this expression to show that you approve of something or are pleased about something.

Rory: The builder said the work on the house is nearly finished. We can move in next week.
Gillian: Good! I'm tired of living in this small flat.

good grief!
You use this expression to show great surprise or shock.
Sally: Good grief! It's been snowing! I've never known it to snow here before.
Meg: And look how deep it is!

good heavens!
You use this expression when you are surprised about something. You can also use *Heavens!* in the same way.
Jane: Good heavens! There's our neighbour over there.
Jim: So it is. Imagine coming halfway across the world and meeting someone we know.

good question!
You use this expression in reply to a question to which it is difficult to find an answer.
Dan: I hear you're going to Jim's wedding in New Zealand next year. How're you going to afford it?
Ken: Good question! I'm hoping to get an evening job to earn some extra money. If not, I might get a loan.

great!
You use this expression to indicate that you are very pleased about something.
Tom: I've found us a flat near the town centre.
Karen: Great! When do we move in? I can't wait to get out of here.

You can also use the expression ironically to indicate that you are not at all pleased about something, but are disappointed, upset, etc.

Harry: The landlord's putting the rent up.
Joe: **Great!** Where am I going to find the extra money? I've just taken out a loan on a car.

hang on!
You use this expression when you want to ask someone to wait for you.
Hannah: I'm just going to the library. I'll see you later.
Rose: **Hang on!** I'll come with you. I've got some books to return.

You can also use this expression to ask someone to stop what they are doing or thinking.
Ben: It must have been Matt who set fire to my garage. He wanted revenge. I'm going to call the police.
John: **Hang on**, Ben. You've no proof it was Matt.

hardly!
You use this expression when something seems very unlikely in your opinion.
Kate: Is Tom taking you to that new French restaurant?
Liz: **Hardly!** He couldn't possibly afford it. It's very expensive.

having said that
You use this expression before you add something that makes what you have said less strong.
Bob: Dave doesn't seem to treat his wife very well. **Having said that**, I don't think she's an easy person to get along with.
Mike: No, she isn't. I think they deserve each other.

heavens! *see* **good heavens!**

heaven knows!
Use this expression to emphasize that you do not know something or that it is difficult to find an answer to something.

Jackie: The landlord's given us a month's notice on our flat. It is such a blow. We've been so happy there.
Mary: Where will you live?
Jackie: **Heaven knows!** Flats are difficult to find around here.

how's it going?
You can use this informal phrase when asking someone how they are.
Ken: Hi, George, **how's it going?**
George: OK. I'm a bit tired because I've been working late every night this week.

I can't tell you
You use this expression when you wish to emphasize what strong feelings you have about something.
Diane: **I can't tell you** how much I appreciate your help. I simply couldn't have coped without it.
Jane: I'm just glad I was able to help.

I can't think why
An everyday expression used to emphasize that you do not understand something at all.
Ben: Jim's decided to leave his job.
Joe: Yes, I heard that, but **I can't think why**. It's a well paid job and he's been so happy there.
Ben: He says he can't stand his new boss.

I could do without
You use this expression when you want to emphasize that you do not want to do something or have someone or something.
Sue: **I could do without** working late tonight. I have guests coming for dinner.
Lucy: I've got to work too and my parents-in-law are coming round to see the kids. They won't be pleased.

I dare say
You use this expression when you want to say that something is probable or likely.
Alicia: **I dare say** Jenny thinks that she's doing the right thing moving in with her parents, but I think she'll regret it. She doesn't get on with them very well.
Diana: Well, she doesn't think she's got a choice. Both her parents have got health problems.

I hate to think
You use this expression when you want to stress how bad you consider a situation is or might be.
Ken: My wife wants us to go on a world cruise when I retire.
Bill: That'll be nice, but **I hate to think** what it'll cost you.

I'm afraid
This expression does not mean that you are feeling fear. You use it when you are apologizing or when you are politely telling someone something that may upset or annoy them.
Ken: Do you have two single rooms for one night?
Hotel receptionist: **I'm afraid** we don't have any vacancies. It's the middle of the tourist season and we're very busy.

Anne: This TV set keeps switching itself on and off. Can you have a look at it?
Repairman: I've had a look and **I'm afraid** I can't repair it. You're going to have to get a new one.

I must say
You use this expression when you want to emphasize how you feel about something or what you think about something.
Fiona: **I must say** that meal was absolutely delicious.
Bob: Yes, it was. And it wasn't very expensive.

I suppose so
You use this expression when you say that you agree with someone but rather reluctantly.
Mark: It's getting late and we're tired. I think we should leave the rest of this job until tomorrow.
Tom: **I suppose so**, but I wish we could have finished it tonight.

I thought as much
You use this expression when you find out that something you suspected turns out to be true.
Derek: It's the cat next door that's been digging up the plants in our front garden. I've just seen it doing it.
Lisa: **I thought as much** but when I spoke to its owner she said it was never out at the front of the house.

I thought I'd
Use this expression when you want to tell someone what you are planning to do.
Janet: What are you going to do on your day off?
Wendy: **I thought I'd** go and look for a present for Sally.
Janet: That's a good idea. I've got to find something as well.

I told you so
You use this expression when you are reminding someone that you had warned them that something bad or unfortunate would happen before it did.
Jim: I wish I hadn't bought this cheap TV. The quality of the picture's terrible.
George: **I told you so**. I said that you only get what you pay for.

if you don't mind my saying so
You use this expression when you are going to say something that criticizes someone in some way or is likely to annoy or upset them.

Mrs Brown: **If you don't mind my saying so**, that child should be in bed by now.

Mrs Smith: It's got nothing to do with you, and anyway she usually goes to bed much earlier than this but we were visiting my mother and we missed the last bus.

I've no idea

You use this expression to emphasize that you do not know anything about something.

Debbie: We've run out of petrol. How far is it to the next town?

Lyn: **I've no idea**, but I'm pretty sure it's too far to walk, especially in these shoes.

Debbie: We'll just have to hope that someone comes along to help.

I was wondering if/whether ... ?

You use this expression as a polite way of asking somebody something.

Sophie: **I was wondering if** I could borrow your laptop this evening for a couple of hours? My computer's being repaired.

Dorothy: Sure! It's on the desk in my study.

it's beyond me

You use this expression when you want to stress that you do not understand something.

Will: My daughter's on the phone again—and to her best friend. **It's beyond me** what they find to say to each other. They're at school together all day.

Ron: My daughter's just the same. She's always on her mobile phone, either talking or texting.

it's just that

You use this expression when you are giving a reason or explanation for something.

Lucy: It's a pity you can't go on holiday with us.

Amy: Yes, I'm so sorry but it can't be helped. **It's just that** I can't get away from the office at that time of year.

it's no big deal
You use this expression to indicate that something is not at all important.
Mary: Thanks very much for offering to help me move all these books.
Bob: **It's no big deal!** I wasn't doing anything else anyway.

let me see/let's see
You use this expression when you are thinking about something.
Tourist: Excuse me, do you know of a good seafood restaurant in this area?
Peter: **Let me see**. There are two or three, but the one I like best is the one down on the shore. It's called the Crab Shell. It's very good.

Tourist: Excuse, me. Can you tell me where the nearest bank is, please?
Bill: **Let's see**. Some of them have closed down recently. The nearest one's in George Street, just off Main Street. Do you know where that is?
Tourist: Yes, I do. Many thanks.

listen
You often use this interjection when you want someone to pay attention or if you want to interrupt someone. It's usually not meant rudely and is often followed by *sorry*.
Salesman: Hello, sir. Can I ask if you've ever thought about the doors and windows in your home and whether ... ?
Tim: **Listen**. Sorry to stop you there, but I am not at all interested in double glazing and I don't want to waste your time.

look!

You use this interjection when you want someone to pay attention to what you are going to say, often when you are annoyed.

Martin: Look! I forgot I was supposed to be meeting you and I've said I'm sorry. What more do you expect me to do?

Tina: You could say sorry as though you meant it.

lookout!

You use this interjection to warn someone of possible danger.

Neil: Lookout! This pavement's very icy.

Caroline: Thanks for the warning. I'll be careful.

me too

You use this expression when you wish to agree with someone or when you wish to be included in something.

Liz: I'm furious that they're pulling down that lovely old building.

Helen: Me too. It's disgraceful. I'm going to organize a protest!

never mind

You use this expression when you want to tell someone that something is not important.

Tara: I broke one of your mugs when I was stacking the dishwasher. Sorry. I'll replace it.

Nancy: Never mind! It wasn't an expensive one and I've got plenty of other mugs.

Nathalie: I'm sorry I can't come to the meeting tonight. I promised to have dinner with my parents.

Jim: Never mind. I'll let you know what happens and you can come to the next one.

no chance!

Use this expression when you think that it is extremely unlikely that something will happen.

Jill: Do you think Tom and Sally will get back together?
Lucy: **No chance!** She said it's definitely over. She discovered he was cheating on her with her best friend.

no fear!

You use this expression in informal contexts to stress that you are definitely not going to do something or that something is not going to happen.

Sarah: Are you going on holiday with your parents?
Tom: **No fear!** They like to wander round museums and old churches. I just want to go and lie on a beach somewhere.

Donald: Will Jim really leave his job do you think? He's always saying he will.
William: **No fear!** He's far too well paid to do that.

no way!

You use this expression to emphasize that you are not going to do something or that something is not likely to happen.

Tom: Are you going to apologize to Anne?
Ryan: **No way!** I didn't do anything wrong.

no wonder

You use this expression when you consider that something is not at all surprising or that it is to be expected.

Harry: Jack's really furious with me.
Charles: **No wonder.** You borrowed his bike without asking him and then damaged it.

Sue: **No wonder** Jane's feeling miserable. Her dog's just died.
Elizabeth: And she adored it. She'd had it since it was a puppy.

not on your life!

You use this expression when you want to stress that you are definitely not going to do something.

Bill: Are you going to help Bob move house tomorrow?
Sam: **Not on your life!** I'm exhausted after a week's hard work. I need a rest. And Bob never does anything to help other people.
Bill: That's true. I don't think I'll help him either.

not to worry/don't worry
You use this expression to show that you do not think that something is important.
Martha: I'm so sorry but I can't come to the cinema tonight. The boss's asked me to work late.
Joe: **Not to worry**. We can go some other time. I'll give you a ring.

oh dear!
Use this expression when you are disappointed, upset or worried.
Kate: **Oh dear!** We've just missed a bus. We'll have to wait an hour for the next one.
Diana: We might as well go and have some coffee. Where's the nearest café?

oops!
You use this expression when you drop something or nearly drop something, when you have made a mistake, or accidentally revealed a secret.
Jessica: **Oops!** I've dropped a contact lens. Can anyone see it?
Paula: There it is, over there. I'll get it.

ouch!
You use this interjection when you feel a sudden pain.
Simon: **Ouch!** I've been stung by a wasp.
Tanya: I'm going inside. I hate wasps.

You might also use *ouch* if someone has hurt your feelings.

Janice: That dress does nothing for you.
Jenny: **Ouch!** At least you're honest, I suppose.

ow!
You can also use this interjection when you feel a sudden pain.
Malcolm: **Ow!** That hurt my arm. Don't throw the ball so hard.
James: Sorry! But you were supposed to catch it.

phew!
This interjection can be used in several situations. You can use it to indicate that you are feeling tired.
Pete: **Phew!** That climb was much harder than I thought.

You can use it to indicate that you are feeling hot.
Alice: **Phew!** I find this heat unbearable. I'm going inside.

You can also use it to indicate that you are feeling very relieved because something did not happen.
Luke: **Phew!** I'm glad the teacher didn't ask me any questions about the play. I haven't read it yet!

quite right too!
You use this expression to emphasize how much you agree with something.
Joan: I'm thinking of moving to a bigger flat. This place is just not big enough.
Catherine: **Quite right too!** You need a lot more space.

rather you than me!
You use this expression to stress that you would certainly not want to be involved in something that someone else is going to do.
Tim: Are you really going to swim in the sea at this time of year? **Rather you than me!** It will be freezing.
Jack: I know, but the others are going to do it and I don't want to look like a coward.

really?
You say this in response to something that you hear that surprises you or interests you very much.
Sarah: I've just met Wendy. She's just got married.
Kate: **Really?** I didn't even know that she was seeing someone.

right you are
This is quite an old-fashioned expression that is used when you agree to do as someone has suggested.
John: I'm going to be a bit late so I won't have time to come for a drink before the meal. I'll meet you at the restaurant.
Martin: **Right you are**, John. See you there.

roll on ... !
You use this expression when you want something that you know you will find pleasant to happen very soon.
Craig: I'm so tired. I've been working late and coming in early every day this week.
Ian: So have I. **Roll on** the weekend so we can get a rest!

same here
You use this expression to indicate that you share someone else's opinion or feelings or that you are in a similar situation to theirs.
Annette: It seems to take me much longer to get to work these days.
Joanne: **Same here**. The traffic's got much worse in the morning for some reason.

search me!
You use this expression when you want to stress that you do not know the answer to a question.
Joe: Why's the boss looking so angry?
Thomas: **Search me!** He's been in a terrible mood all morning but I can't think why.
Joe: Maybe he's had a row with his wife.

shh!
You use this expression to ask someone to be quiet or make less noise.
Molly: Shh! I've just got the baby to sleep.
Mark: Sorry. I hope I didn't wake her.

shoo!
You use this interjection to tell an animal or someone who is annoying you to go away.
Donald: There's that cat again from across the road. I'm going to try and get rid of it. **Shoo!**
Robbie: It'll just come back again. It seems to like your garden more than its own!

so what?
This expression is rather rude. You use it when you think that something someone has said is not relevant or important.
Sally: You were a bit late getting to the students' meeting.
Pamela: So what? These meetings are a complete waste of time. I wish I hadn't bothered to go at all.

so what's new?
You use this expression in an informal context to stress that you do not think that something is at all surprising or unexpected.
Craig: My computer's crashed again.
Ken: So what's new? It's always breaking down. You need to get a new one. That one's ancient!

some hope!
You use this expression to emphasize that you think that there is very little, or no, chance of something happening.
Jackie: Do you think there's any chance we'll get a pay raise this year?
Monica: Some hope! Sales are down and profits are at an all-time low. We'll be lucky if we get to keep our jobs.

speaking of

You use this expression when you want to say something more about a person or thing that has just been mentioned.

Debbie: Sue won't be at work this week. She's on holiday.

Mary: **Speaking of** holidays, are you still thinking of going to Australia this year?

Debbie: Yes. I'm going to visit my sister.

suit yourself!

You use this expression rather rudely to tell someone that they can do what they want to do when you are annoyed with them for not doing what you want them to do.

Helen: Jill's having a party tonight. Do you want to come with me?

Rose: Sorry, I can't. I've an English essay to finish.

Helen: **Suit yourself!** I'll get Anne to come but it would do you good to have some fun for a change.

sure!

You use this expression when you mean *yes* or *yes, certainly.*

Jim: Are you going to work by car today?

Adam: Yes. I'm just about to leave.

Jim: Could you possibly give me a ride? My car won't start and I need to be at work for an important meeting.

Adam: **Sure!** Come round right away.

talk about ... !

You say *talk about* ... when you want to emphasize something.

Carole: **Talk about** stinginess! Joe's just asked me for the money for the coffee he bought me yesterday.

Laura: That's typical of him!

that's all I need!

You use this expression when a problem or difficulty arises when you are already having several other problems or difficulties to cope with.

Jerry: **That's all I need!**
Bill: What's wrong?
Jerry: My car won't start and the boss has just rung to say he needs me in the office right away. Before that I spilled coffee on my shirt and had to change it and then I slipped on the stairs and hurt my ankle.
Bill: Calm down! You can come in my car. I work quite near you.
Jerry: Thanks!

that's fine by me
You use this expression when you are indicating that you agree to do something which has been suggested.
Peter: The film starts very early. We could go to the cinema first and eat later.
Alicia: **That's fine by me**. I'm not very hungry, anyway.

that's news to me
You use this expression when you hear about something that you did not know, often when you feel that you should have known about it earlier.
Ben: Apparently they're going to renovate our office and we need to move while the work gets done.
Garth: **That's news to me**. Who told you?
Ben: The office manager.
Garth: Well, she should have told me as well. I've got a lot of stuff to move.

that's OK with me
You use this expression when you are indicating that you agree to something which has been suggested.
Lisa: We're going to have to go by train. My car's broken down and they can't repair it till tomorrow.
Maria: **That's OK with me**. I love going by train and I sometimes get sick in a car.

that's too bad
You use this expression when you want to say that something is unfortunate.
Hugh: The picnic's been cancelled because of the rain.
Lisa: **That's too bad**. The kids will be upset. They were really looking forward to it.
Hugh: We're organizing some indoor games for them. That should cheer them up!

there's no doubt about it
You use this expression to emphasize that something is definitely true or certain.
Frank: I can't believe that Bob would steal money from the company. He seems such an honest guy.
Mike: It does seem amazing, but **there's no doubt about it**. The police have proof and Bob has confessed. Apparently, he has huge gambling debts and stole the money to pay them off.

there you go/are
You use this expression when you are giving something to someone or have done something for them.
Customer: A kilo of red apples, please.
Shopkeeper: **There you go**. A kilo of my very best apples. Enjoy.
Customer: Thank you.

though
You use this word at the end of a sentence when you want to make the previous statement less strong or less important.
Ken: I've got to work on Saturday. It's annoying because I'd made plans. I've got an extra two days off next week, **though**.
John: That's not too bad. It's good to get some time off during the week sometimes.

too true!
You use this expression when you want to stress how true you consider a statement to be or how much you agree with it.

Trisha: It's time that women factory workers got the same pay as the men.
Patsy: **Too true!** After all, they're doing the same kind of work.

Jane: It's so cold in this office. They should really put the heating on.
Betty: **Too true!** My hands are freezing. I can scarcely work my keyboard.

tut!/tut,tut!
You use this sound to show that you disapprove of something. It is often used humorously.
Mrs Brown: **Tut!** Look at what those children are doing. They're disturbing everyone. You'd think their parents would stop them.
Mrs Smith: They're not paying any attention to them. Some parents just don't care.

Bob: **Tut, tut!** What are you doing here, Jennifer? Aren't you meant to be at work?
Jennifer: No, I took the day off to come to the fair. How about you, Bob?
Bob: I've just come for an hour. It's my lunch break.

ugh!
You use this expression to show that you dislike something very much or that it disgusts you.
Alison: **Ugh!** This sauce has mushrooms in it. I hate them!
Barbara: I think it's delicious.

uh-huh
You make this sound when you are agreeing with someone or saying *yes*.
Barry: Are you going to Pam's party tonight? Most of our friends are going.
Susan: **Uh-huh**, but I might be a bit late.

what about?
You use this expression when you are making a suggestion to someone about something.
Alex: I've had a hard day at the office. I quite fancy going out.
Meg: Me, too. **What about** going to the cinema?
Alex: Good idea! I'll see what's on.

what about it?/how about it?
You use this expression in an informal context when you are asking someone if they agree with a suggestion that you have made.
Lucy: You can have my spare room for a month if you give me some help with childcare. **What about it?**
Alice: Yes, thanks. It will be great to have somewhere to stay until I can move into my new flat.

what did I tell you?
You use this expression after you have warned someone that something bad or unfortunate might happen and it does happen.
Patrick: Sally's just found out that her new boyfriend is married with two children.
Luke : **What did I tell you?** I said there was something deceitful about him.

what if?
You use this expression when you want to mention something that might happen, especially something bad or unhelpful.
Tom: We have to change planes in London and we don't have much time between the flights.
Pete: **What if** we miss our connection?
Tom: We'll just have to hope that we don't.

what's more
You use this expression when you wish to add something to what you have just said, often something very important or relevant.

Pam: I'm not taking a holiday this year. I'm very busy at work and, **what's more**, I can't really afford to go away.
Tessa: Neither can I. I've just spent a lot of money on the house.

what's the use?
You use this expression when you want to stress that doing or saying something will have no effect.
Harry: I should try to warn Sue that Bill's not to be trusted.
Wendy: **What's the use?** She wouldn't believe you. She's madly in love with him.
Harry: She's going to get hurt.
Wendy: Well, there's nothing we can do.

what's up?
You use this expression to find out if something bad or unfortunate has happened. You can add *with* to find out why someone is upset.
Jack: The local shop's not open. **What's up?**
Sally: There was a break-in last night and the owner got hurt.
Jack: Poor man. Is he going to be all right?
Sally: He's fine, but he's in shock. The shop'll be closed for the rest of the week at least.

why don't ... ?
Use this expression to make suggestions.
Larry: It's a glorious day. **Why don't** we go to the beach?
Peggy: Good idea. I'll go and put a picnic together.
Larry: And I'll take the car to get more petrol.

wonders will never cease!
You use this expression when you want to express great surprise. It is often used ironically.
Myra: **Wonders will never cease!** I actually found a parking place in the town centre.
Jane: You were lucky! Parking there's getting more and more impossible.

wouldn't you know it?

You use this expression when something unexpected has happened and caused problems or difficulties for you. Sometimes the expression is *wouldn't you just know it?*

Mark: **Wouldn't you know it?** I usually arrive early at the station and the train is usually late. Today I was slightly later and the train was early.

Joe: Did you miss it?

Mark: Yes, the train was just leaving the platform as I got there.

you could always

You use this expression when you are making a suggestion to someone. Other personal pronouns, such as I, he, she, or a noun can be used instead of *you*.

Will: The last train leaves quite early in the evening but **you could always** stay tonight with me and get the first train in the morning. It leaves very early.

Sam: Thanks for the invitation. I think I might just do that.

you'll never guess!

You use this expression when you are about to tell someone something very surprising or exciting.

Sally: **You'll never guess** who I've just seen!

Anne: I can't think who. Why don't you tell me?

Sally: It was Rob Brown.

Anne: I thought he was in prison for fraud.

Sally: He was but he's out. It seems he was innocent all along.

you never know

You use this expression when you think that it is just possible that something might happen, although it is very unlikely.

Alan: **You never know**. Mike might pass the English exam, although he's not very good at English and some of the questions were very difficult.

Dave: I would be very surprised if he passed. He didn't do much studying for it.

yuck!

You use this expression to indicate that something tastes unpleasant or disgusting.

Mary: **Yuck!** This soup has far too much salt in it.

Jade: So it does. It tastes horrible.

Homophones

A homophone is a word that is pronounced the same as another word but it differs in meaning or spelling or both. A few examples are listed below.

ail, a rather old-fashioned verb meaning to be ill, as in *The old woman is ailing*; or to be the matter, to be wrong, as in *What ails you?*
ale, a noun meaning a kind of beer, as in *a pint of foaming ale*.

alter a verb meaning to change, as in *They have had to alter their plans*.
altar a noun meaning, in the Christian church, the table on which the bread and wine are consecrated for communion and which serves as the centre of worship, as in *The priest moved to the altar, from where he dispensed communion*. The word can also refer to a raised structure on which sacrifices are made, as in *The Druids made sacrifices on the altar of their gods*.

blew a verb, the past tense of the verb to blow, as in *They blew the trumpets loudly*.
blue a noun and adjective meaning a colour of the shade of a clear sky, as in *She wore a blue dress*.

boar a noun meaning a male pig, as in *a dish made with wild boar*.
bore a verb meaning to produce a hole in something with a drill as in *He bored a hole in the wall*.
bore a verb meaning to make tired and uninterested, as in *The audience was obviously bored by the rather academic lecture*.
bore a verb, the past tense of the verb to bear, as in *They bore their troubles lightly*.

cereal a noun meaning a plant yielding grain suitable for food, as in *Countries which grow cereal crops* and *Quite a lot of cereal crops are grown in the UK* and a prepared food made with grain, as in *We often have cereal for breakfast.*

serial a noun meaning a story or television play which is published or appears in regular parts, as in *the final instalment of the magazine serial which she was following.*

cite a verb meaning to quote or mention by way of example or proof, as in *The lawyer cited a previous case to try and get his client off a charge of manslaughter.*

sight a noun meaning the act of seeing, as in *They recognized him at first sight.*

site a noun meaning a location, place, as in *They have found a site for the new factory.*

feat a noun meaning a notable act or deed, as in *The old man received an award for his courageous feat.*

feet a noun, the plural form of *foot*, as in *The child got her feet wet from walking through a puddle.*

know a verb meaning to have understanding or knowledge of, as in *He is the only one who knows the true facts of the situation,* and *to be acquainted with*, as in *I met her once but I don't really know her.*

no an adjective meaning not any, as in *We have no food left* and *There is no right of way through the large estate.*

none a pronoun meaning not any, as in *They are demanding money but we have none.*

nun a noun meaning a woman who joins a religious order and takes vows of poverty, chastity and obedience, as in *She gave up the world to become a nun.*

rite a noun meaning a ceremonial act or words, as in *She has been taking part in rites involving witchcraft.*

right an adjective meaning correct, as in *Very few people gave the right answer to the question.*

write a verb meaning to form readable characters, as in *He writes regularly for the newspapers.*

stare a verb and noun meaning to look fixedly and a fixed gaze, as in *She stared at him in disbelief when he told her the news* and *He gave me an angry stare.*

stair a noun meaning a series of flights of steps, as in *The old lady caught her foot on the stair.*

Homonyms

A homonym is one of a group of words that share the same spelling and the same pronunciation but have different meanings. A few examples are listed below.

bank a noun meaning an institution offering financial services, such as the safekeeping of money and lending of money, as in *I have opened a savings account at the bank*.
bank a noun meaning a long raised mass, a hill or a slope and especially the sloping sides of a river, as in *We walked for miles along the banks of the river*.

bill a noun meaning a written statement of money owed, as in *You must pay the telephone bill immediately*.
bill a noun meaning a bird's beak, as in *The seagull has injured its bill*.

fair an adjective meaning attractive, as in *fair young women*; light in colour, as in *She has fair hair*; fine, not raining, as in *I hope it keeps fair*; just, free from prejudice, as in *We felt that the referee came to a fair decision*.
fair a noun which formerly meant a market held regularly in the same place, often with stalls, entertainments and rides but now referring more to an event with entertainments and rides without the market, as in *He won a coconut at the fair*; a trade exhibition, as in *the Frankfurt Book Fair*.

pulse a noun meaning the throbbing caused by the contractions of the heart, as in *The patient has a weak pulse*.
pulse a noun meaning the edible seeds of any of various crops of the pea family, such as lentils, peas and beans, as in *Vegetarians eat a lot of food made with pulses*.

row a verb, pronounced to rhyme with **low**, meaning to propel a boat by means of oars, as in *He plans to row across the Atlantic single-handed*.

row a noun, pronounced to rhyme with **low**, meaning a number of people or things arranged in a line, as in *We tried to get into the front row to watch the procession*.

trip a noun meaning a tour, journey or a voyage, as in *I had a wonderful time during my trip to Spain*.

trip a verb meaning to stumble or fall over something, as in *I tripped over a fallen branch in the wood and twisted my ankle*.

Homographs and heteronyms

A homograph is one of a group of words that are spelled the same way but have different meanings.

A homograph that is also pronounced differently is a heteronym. Some examples of heteronyms are given below.

bow pronounced to rhyme with **how**, a verb meaning to bend the head or body as a sign of respect or in greeting as in *The visitors bowed to the emperor* and *The mourners bowed their heads as the coffin was lowered into the grave*.

bow pronounced to rhyme with **low**, a noun meaning a looped knot or a ribbon tied in this way, as in *She wears blue bows in her hair*; or a wooden tool used to propel an arrow, as in *He shot the arrow from the bow*.

deliberate pronounced to rhyme with **deliber-at**, an adjective meaning carefully thought out or planned, intentional, as in *It was a deliberate insult*.

deliberate pronounced to rhyme with **deliber-ate**, a verb meaning to consider something deeply, to ponder or think something over, as in *The jury deliberated for some time before reaching a verdict*.

lead pronounced **leed**, a verb meaning to show the way, as in *The guide will lead you down the mountain*.

lead pronounced **led**, a noun meaning a type of greyish metal, as in *They are going to remove water pipes made from lead*.

row pronounced to rhyme with **low**, a noun meaning a number of people or things arranged in a line, as in *The princess sat in the front row*.

row pronounced to rhyme with **how**, a noun meaning a quarrel, a disagreement, as in *He has had a row with his neighbour over repairs to the garden wall*.

sow pronounced to rhyme with **low**, a verb meaning to scatter seeds in the earth, as in *She sowed some flower seeds in the garden*.

sow pronounced to rhyme with **how**, a noun meaning a female pig, as in *The sow is in her pigsty with her piglets*.

In conclusion

Improving your written and spoken English is not as difficult or boring as you might think now that you have a better understanding of English grammar. Improving your personal writing style and word power is even less difficult. Writing in English, in particular, gives you the opportunity to practise your language skills and make good use of your knowledge of English grammar and it can be fun as well as rewarding. Try it and see!